Cranberry Cooking
For All Seasons

Design by Hannah Haines and Joseph D. Thomas

Text ©2002 Nancy Cappelloni

    Library of Congress Cataloging-in-Publication Data

Cappelloni, Nancy.
 Cranberry cooking for all seasons / by Nancy Cappelloni.
   p. cm.
   ISBN 0-932027-71-7 (pbk.)
   1. Cookery (Cranberries) I. Title.
   TX813.C7 C37 2002
   641.6'476--dc21
                   2002014559

Cranberry Cooking
For All Seasons

by

Nancy Cappelloni

Spinner Publications, Inc.
New Bedford, Massachusetts

Acknowledgments

To my husband, Bob, and to my daughters Lauren, Lisa and Dana for your continued encouragement, constant caring and for enjoying all the cranberry dishes I prepared for you.

I would like to recognize, with sincerest thanks and gratitude:

My family and friends, who tested and critiqued my recipes.

My cousin, Richie for inspiring me in the kitchen through his joy of cooking.

My mother for showing me the importance of food in our family.

The professional chefs and home cooks who shared their stories and recipes, including the Iroquois Cranberry Growers, the Nantucket Island Chamber of Commerce and Drew Spangler.

The Cape Cod Cranberry Growers Association, Ocean Spray Cranberries, Plimoth Plantation, *Cranberries Magazine* and The Cranberry Institute for sharing their knowledge and research with me.

Ruth Caswell and Janice Anderson Gram for their wisdom and support.

The Wampanoag Tribe of Aquinnah, with special thanks to Helen Manning and Gladys Widdiss for their inspiration.

All the cranberry growers in North America.

Joe Thomas, my publisher, for believing in this project and the tremendous editorial efforts of everyone at Spinner Publications.

Thank you.

— *Nancy Cappelloni*

Credits

The publishers wish to thank Greater New Bedford Regional Vocational Technical High School for use of their Culinary Arts facility to prepare and photograph all of the food images. Thanks to chef Henry Bousquet of Four Corners Caterers and the Vocational students for their fine work in cooking and presenting the meals. Thanks also to our staff, friends and volunteers:

Jay Avila, electronic imaging
Ruth Caswell, copy-editing
Cerulli's Gourmet Foods
Decas Brothers Cranberries
Sharon Georgianna
James Grasela, copy-editing
Hannah Haines, design
Marsha L. McCabe, editing

Kerry Downey Romaniello, proof-reading
John K. Robson, photography
Tim Sylvia, photography
Andrea V. Tavares, copy-editing
Anne J. Thomas, proof-reading
Joseph D. Thomas, photography/design
UMass Cranberry Experiment Station

Special Thanks to

The Cape Cod Cranberry Growers' Association

for their generous support

The Cape Cod Cranberry Growers' Association is one of the oldest farmers organizations in the country. Established in 1888 to standardize the measure with which cranberries are sold (the 100 lb. barrel), it has become one of the leading agricultural organizations in Massachusetts. In 1888 the Association's mission was "to promote the interest of its members in whatever pertains to the growth, cultivation and sale of cranberries."

Although a great deal has changed in cranberry farming since the Association began, today's cranberry growers still face many challenges. Through a unified voice the CCCGA works to promote the cranberry industry through active grower volunteer committees in Public Relations and Promotions, Government Affairs, Research and Environmental Affairs.

The CCCGA has a professional staff that assists growers in solving everyday problems, offering assistance in regulatory compliance, sponsoring professional development seminars and organizing association activities such as the Massachusetts Cranberry Harvest Festival every Columbus Day weekend. The CCCGA also operates a frost warning system. In the event of frost danger, cranberry grower members are notified by a personal phone call or through access to a special code-a-phone.

The CCCGA has invested over $500,000 in cranberry research to help improve the efficiency and environmental compatibility of cranberry farms. Over 450 cranberry farmers belong to the CCCGA today. Membership in CCCGA is voluntary and based on a per barrel assessment.

Through continued grower support, CCCGA is working to ensure that cranberry farming can survive urbanization and that open space and clean water, vital to cranberry growing, will be preserved.

Financial support for this project was provided in part through the Massachusetts Department of Food and Agriculture's Agricultural Specialty Crop Funds.

Contents

Desserts

Breads, Scones, Coffee Cakes and Muffins

Beverages

To the Children of the Earth *wutche'wusgkowan*

by Nancy Eldredge, Penobscot/Wampanoag, 1992

Let every day
be one of giving thanks–
Let every being and creature
along our paths be appreciated–
Let all plant life be acknowledged–
Let all the winged ones of the air
know your gratefulness.
Great spirit–

    Thank you for all that is

    For all that we take,

    we will give

    at least, our acknowledgment

    Thank you for every mountain and

    every grain of sand

Water and Air
Fire and Earth
For every living thing
And for the beauty of our lives this day,
We thank you.

Introduction

Cranberries are becoming the trendiest of fruits, not only because they're beautiful and tasty, but they're just what the doctor ordered. Cranberries are high in Vitamin C, free of fat and cholesterol, low in calories and sodium, and relatively high in fiber. Researchers around the world are finding components in cranberries linked to the prevention of numerous infections and diseases. And it makes good food sense. Sweet or tart, jellied or whole, in breads, sauces or desserts, the cranberry is as versatile and tasty as it is healthy.

The cranberry is an important ingredient in American history, also. As one of America's native fruits (along with the Concord grape and the blueberry), cranberries nourished the Native American Indians living along the Eastern woodlands, hundreds of years before explorers and settlers touched foot in the New World. With the help of their Indian friends, the new settlers quickly discovered the culinary possibilities and medicinal properties of wild cranberries.

From September through December, when they are harvested and placed fresh on the market, cranberries have always been a popular ingredient in American cooking. Today, of course, cranberries are available all year—juiced, dried, and frozen. They have long since broken out of their traditional role as a Thanksgiving and Christmas holiday condiment. A trip down the aisles of your local grocery store will reveal cranberries in juices, health drinks, baked goods and mixes, cereals, cookies, salad dressings and marinades.

Though the cranberry has found its way into many cookbooks, it generally plays a background role. *Cranberry Cooking for All Seasons* is unique because the cranberry is the star. Besides offering you the best cranberry recipes on earth, you will learn about cranberry history, legend and folklore, as well as harvesting, production and cooking.

Home cooks at all skill levels will find *Cranberry Cooking for All Seasons* appealing for its easy-to-follow, intriguing array of recipes. If you're a professional chef or culinary researcher; if you're a health nut and always on the lookout for salubrious recipes; or, if you love cranberries and simply want more recipes, welcome to cranberry paradise.

— *Spinner Publications, Inc.*

Cranberries on the vines. — *National Archives photograph.*

The American Cranberry

by Nancy Cappelloni

GROWING THE CRANBERRY

The cranberry most often used in commercial cultivation in North America is an eye-popping red, sour, round berry. A native wetland crop, it thrives in a rare combination of conditions—sandy soil, a favorable climate and proper underlying geology. Its botanical name is Vaccinium macrocarpon from the Heath family Ericaceae.

This trailing woody vine produces stems or "runners" from one to six-feet long. The runners sprout short little branches about two or three inches long called "uprights," on which pale rose flowers form buds. Most of the berries, borne by blossoms on the uprights, are round and turn red in early fall. During the growing season, from April to November, the leaves are a dark glossy green, then a reddish brown in the dormant season.

Cranberries grow on low-lying vines in beds, commonly known as bogs or marshes, which result from glacial deposits that left impermeable kettle holes lined with clay. These beds became filled with water and decaying matter, creating an ideal environment for cranberries. Cranberries can only grow and survive under a very special combination of factors: they require an acid peat soil, a fresh water supply and a prolonged growing season. Besides the bog, cranberry growth relies on a surrounding network of fields, forests, streams and ponds, which make up the cranberry wetlands system.

Cranberry vines need not be re-planted as they will survive indefinitely if they are undamaged. More than 100 varieties of cranberries grow in North America, chiefly the "Ben Lear," "Early Black," "Howes," "McFarlin," "Pilgrim," "Searles" and "Stevens." In Massachusetts, some vines are over 150 years old and still bear fruit.

In contrast to its cultivated kin, the wild American cranberry is a trailing evergreen vine found as far north as Newfoundland, west to Minnesota, and south to the higher elevations of North Carolina.

Naming the Cranberry

A graceful water bird appears to play a part in the naming of the cranberry. One theory suggests that Dutch and German settlers called the fruit "crane-berry," having observed it to be a favorite food of cranes. Another theory suggests the slender stem and downward hanging blossom, resembling the head and neck of an English crane, gave rise to the name "crane-berry," which was later shortened to "cranberry."

The Indian tribes of the Woodland region gave different names to the wild cranberry, based on their diverse languages stemming from the Proto-Algonquian culture. The Wampanoag of eastern Massachusetts called the berry "sassamenesh," meaning very sour berry. The Cape Cod Pequot and Leni-Lenape tribes of New Jersey, Delaware, southeast New York and eastern Pennsylvania called the cranberry "ibimi," meaning bitter berry or bitter fruit. The Algonquians of Wisconsin used "atoqua," the Chippewa tribes "anibimin" and the Narragansett's "saytaash." The Indians of the Columbia River region called the cranberry "soolabich."

According to Wampanoag legend, the cranberry was brought from heaven in the beak of a white dove as a gift from the Great Spirit. The dove dropped the berries into a bog where they flourished under the care of Granny Squanit, or Squauanit, the traditional women's god or spiritual guardian who ensured the survival of the many wild fruits and herbs they depended upon. In the fall, when the cranberries around Aquinnah, Martha's Vineyard (formerly Gay Head) were ripe, a young boy would leave a basket of food in the hollows among the sand dunes as a tribute to Granny Squanit.

European settlers created their own version of how the cranberry first came to Massachusetts. An Indian medicine man and an early Christian missionary were arguing over who was most powerful. The Indian cast a spell and mired the Reverend Richard Bourne in quicksand. The two men agreed to a fifteen-day battle of wits. Bourne promised if he lost, he would serve the medicine man, but if he won, he must be fed. Unable to move, Bourne was kept alive by a white dove, which periodically flew down from heaven and fed him a succulent berry. On one occasion, the dove dropped its berry. When the medicine man

Reverend Bourne's respite.
— Pen and ink by Robert A. Henry.

spotted the berry, he realized the dove was feeding Bourne and he tried unsuccessfully to cast a spell on the dove. Finally, the medicine man fell to the ground, exhausted from his own lack of food and water, and the spell on the Reverend Bourne was released. The berry that had fallen to the ground took root and thus began Cape Cod's wild cranberry bogs.

The Indians of the Woodland Region and The Wampanoag

The first North American Indians encountered by the early explorers and settlers were tribes of the Woodland region, which extended south from Canada to the Gulf of Mexico, and west from the Atlantic Ocean to the Mississippi River. The traditional practices of each tribe were distinct, even speaking different languages. In the northeast, farmers and hunters lived in small villages scattered throughout the forests. Their environment supplied them with a plentitude of wildlife, fish, shellfish, wild game, wild berries and nuts. Corn, squash and beans grew in the fertile soil. Maple syrup was tapped from maple trees in some areas. The forests also provided them with resources and materials for their tools, canoes, cooking implements, weapons, clothing and homes. The tribes had a solid botanical knowledge of the plants and their properties. They knew where to find plants with the most desired properties, which parts of the plants to pick and when, how best to preserve them, prepare the medicines, and deliver the most effective doses. When gathering medicinal plants, only a few could be taken from a patch. The rule was to leave a growing plant.

The Wampanoag people inhabited the region of southern New England for more than 12,000 years, thus evolving countless hunting, fishing and food gathering strategies. Managing abundant wild resources, they moved to horticulture and pottery more than 3,000 years ago. The Wampanoag, called "Eastern People," "People of the Light," "People of The First Light" or "People of the Dawn" lived by hunting, gathering, farming and fishing. In the many villages, the people drew what they needed from the land without ever exploiting the resources.

That respect for nature's bounty was passed down through the generations. Gladys Widdiss, Wampanoag elder from Aquinnah, remembers, "When we were youngsters growing up, we ate anything and everything that grew, from the time it sprouted until the time it became food, whatever it was." Only the amount that was needed was harvested.

In the spring, the early tribes moved their villages to the seashore to fish and plant crops. They gathered spring shoots and roots, flowers, fruit, berries, nuts, acorns and various leaves. In the fall and winter, the Wampanoag moved inland to the forests of oak, maple and pine where they hunted deer, wolf, bear, beaver, moose, wild turkey, otter and wildcat. They fished the streams, rivers, lakes and ocean. In winter their diet was largely dependent on what they had stored, though they caught fish through holes in the ice.

Woodlands Indians hunting at Sconticut Neck, Fairhaven, MA. — Illustration by Robert A. Henry, 1984.

During the summer and fall when fruits and berries were harvested, they were dried whole or prepared in small cakes to be used during the winter months in cooking and trading. The "three sisters"—corn, beans and squash were planted together by the Wampanoag women. Corn, the primary crop, was easily dried and stored. Deer was the most important meat source.

The decline of the Wampanoag tribe began before the Pilgrims arrived, devastated by diseases brought over by European explorers in the late fifteenth and early sixteenth centuries, as well as from losses sustained in war. As the English arrived, they created laws stating that unoccupied lands were not owned and quickly expropriated much of the coastal land. The Wampanoag believed in commonly held land and private ownership conflicted with these beliefs.

DISCOVERING CRANBERRIES, "A DELICATE DISH"

The Wampanoag picked sassamanesh (sour berry) from an abundant natural supply, which grew wild in sandy bogs along the coast. The berries became a tasty ingredient in breads, ground or mashed with cornmeal. *Pemmican* was a cake made of fat, dried deer, bear or moose meat and fresh cranberries pounded together, then dried in the sun for later use. A staple food, pemmican provided proteins and vitamins through the winter and on long trips. Cranberries were also boiled in combination with other foods.

During the winter the Wampanoag lived mostly on food that was dried and stored in pits, located near and inside their weetoos (huts). The lined pits, which were dug by the women, were carefully filled with dried cranberries, other fruits and berries, nuts and meats, then topped with mats and covered with earth. Roger Williams observed how the Narragansett took the dried berries called sautaash, beat them to a powder and mixed them with parched corn to make "sautauthig", "…a delicate dish…which is as sweet to them as plum or spice cake to the English."

The Wampanoag knew the healing virtue of cranberries and used them for internal and external treatments. Medicine men brewed them to make poultices to draw poison from arrow wounds. Cranberries were used in tea, believed to calm the nerves. The red dye produced by cranberries was used to color wool and the dried plants were used in the making of rugs and blankets.

Other Northeastern tribes used the leaves of the high bush cranberry as a lotion to treat venereal disease. A tea made from dried leaves acted as a diuretic and cleansed the urinary tract. According to Erichsen-Brown in *Medicinal and other uses of North American Plants,* as early as 1708 and as late as 1915, the Penobscot and Malecite tribes cooked cranberries for medicinal purposes: "They make a conserve of them and esteem them for medicine for stomach problems…. The High-bush cranberries are steeped and drunk for swollen glands and mumps. Plant is boiled and the mess rubbed in the eyes for sore eyes."

Many Eastern Woodland Indians added maple sugar to cranberries, other wild berries, roots and nuts. As noted by John Heckwelder, in 1819: "They make an excellent preserve from the cranberry and crab-apple, to which, after it has been well stewed, they add a proper quantity of sugar or molasses." To create their sweetener, the Indians gathered the sweet sap of the flourishing family of maple trees (called "sheesheegummawis," meaning sap flows fast), and boiled it down to a syrup. They collected the watery liquid and then placed it in a pot of bark or clay. Hot rocks were dropped into the sap to cook it down to a thick, deep brown syrup, or finally, to sugar. They also tapped wild cherry, box elder, birch, beech, hickories and other sap bearing trees.

This late winter harvest produced rich rewards, and the oral traditions of many tribes spread this knowledge. The Mohican Indians believed the melting snow caused the spring sap to run in the maples. Whole Indian families and clans would move to their "sugar bush"—sugar maple groves—for the sweet late-winter labor of sugaring. This lasted from three to six weeks, until the maple trees had budded and blossomed and the clear sap had turned to pale amber.

Maple sugar was also mixed with parched corn and carried in small leather pouches and eaten plain, boiled or mixed with water or fruit juices. The colonists learned to tap the maple trees from the Woodland regional tribes and began storing the maple sugar in wooden tubs to use year-round. They bored a hole in the maple tree to drain the sap, then plugged up the hole with wood from the same tree so it could be tapped over again. Since white sugar was not available until around 1650, and was very expensive, maple sugaring became common practice among New Englanders throughout the 18th century.

THE WAMPANOAG OF AQUINNAH AND CRANBERRY DAY

The Wampanoag people lived for 10,000-12,000 years on Aquinnah, a 3,400-acre peninsula on the southwestern end of Martha's Vineyard, Massachusetts. Aquinnah means "the end of the island." Pursuing a traditional economy based on fishing and agriculture, the Wampanoag shared their resources with European settlers, a fact documented from the early 1600s.

The Wampanoag survived on Noepe, "the dry place," though many members were decimated by disease brought over by the early settlers. The tribe had always held land in common, and this included the cranberry bogs. In 1987, the Aquinnah Wampanoag received

After picking berries in the sand dunes in the Lobsterville section of Aquinnah (Gay Head), Martha's Vineyard, a family of Wampanoag celebrate Cranberry Day with a clam boil, 1989.

John K. Robson photograph

tribal recognition and settlement of long-standing land claims by the federal government. What was left of their common land, including the cranberry bogs, Lobsterville and the Gayhead Cliffs was returned to them. Today, about 300 tribal members live on the Island and care for 477 acres of ancestral land. Wild cranberries still grow on 200 of those acres.

A long-time tradition and important holiday for the Aquinnah Wampanoag is Cranberry Day. Beginning as a week-long encampment at the dunes of Lobsterville, it later became a three-day festival. Today, Cranberry Day is a major one-day celebration, the second Tuesday of October, a symbol of the tribe's revitalized spirit— embodying the spiritual, cultural and political renaissance of the tribe. It is also one of many thanksgiving celebrations held throughout the year, a day of prayer and giving thanks to the Creator. Recognized by the local government as a holiday, Wampanoag children are excused from school to harvest and picnic on their tribal land, one of the last wild cranberry bogs left in this country.

On Cranberry Day, picking begins when the cranberry agent declares the bogs open, usually around 6:00 AM. At 9:00 AM, everyone gathers for the harvest. Traditionally, families bring picnic baskets and food is shared with all. According to Helen Manning, Aquinnah Wampanoag elder, the afternoon is filled with games and storytelling and children listen intensely to the legends told by their elders. The evening ends with a community potluck dinner and singing and dancing.

Gladys Widdiss, an Aquinnah Wampanoag elder, recalls how her parents came to the bogs in oxcarts and gathered cranberries by the bushel. "We picked for two or three days, enough for

A Wampanoag couple at Aquinnah gather berries near the dunes at Lobsterville, Martha's Vineyard, circa 1930.

Spinner Collection

what we figured we needed through the winter, and more. While waiting for our elders to finish picking in the afternoon, we raced cranberries down the dunes, making a trough from the top of the dunes to the bottom; sometimes snake-like, sometimes straight. We'd set the cranberries in a line at the top, push them to start and see whose reached the bottom first."

The men took the harvested cranberries by fishing boats to New Bedford and exchanged them for flour, sugar and molasses. Helen Manning remembers arriving at the bogs in oxcarts and filling them with cranberries, which were stored for the remainder of the year. Her friend's house contained a whole room for storing cranberries picked these few days. Without central heating, the house stayed cool. "As a young boy, my father liked to go into the room and hear the popping sound as he stepped on the cranberries. The cranberries were used for very simple recipes such as cranberry dumplings, cranberry sauce and cranberry cobbler. Everyone had a cow then," Helen recalled," so the cobbler would be served with fresh cream."

Gladys Widdiss recalls, "In my family, after we picked the cranberries, they were poured on the upper level of our homestead, and my grandfather would put in boards so they wouldn't roll out. Those cranberries would stay there all winter and when we children felt bad we'd go up there and run though the cranberries to hear them crack."

The Wampanoag have chosen not to weed, fertilize or tamper with the 200 acres of dunes and cranberry bogs they control. Gladys Widdiss explains, "We say, let the Great Spirit take care of them. Some years we have a lot of cranberries, some years we don't have as many."

PILGRIMS' ARRIVAL

On September 6, 1620, 102 people boarded the *Mayflower* in Plymouth, England and crossed the ocean in search of religious freedom in the New World. On November 9, they sought shelter along the tip of Cape Cod (now Provincetown) but could not find a promising place to settle. They continued to sail, and on December 11 (or 21) they landed at Plymouth Rock and established a settlement. When winter came, food supplies dwindled and the Pilgrims, who knew little about hunting and fishing, were starving. By spring, only 57 Pilgrims and half the crew had survived. The survivors began planting seeds they had brought from home and they continued to build homes.

Samoset, a Pemaquid Indian Chief from the coast of what is now Maine, walked into the Pilgrims' village one day in April and welcomed them in broken English, which he had learned from English fishermen. Days later, he returned to Plymouth with Tisquantum

Massasoit at Plymouth, MA.

John K. Robson photograph

(nicknamed Squanto by William Bradford) who
spoke better English. Squanto was a sole sur-
vivor of the Pawtuxet, a Wampanoag tribe. He
had been kidnapped by the English and taken to
London. Tisquantum informed the Pilgrims that
the Wampanoag chief, Massasoit, the sachem of
Pokanoket, near Bristol, Rhode Island, wanted
to speak with them. Massasoit had alliances with

*Native Americans instruct settlers on farming techniques.
— From Ebenezer W. Pierce:* Indian History…, *1878.*

other Wampanoag villages and these made up the Wampanoag Confederacy. Though there were
many villages besides the Pokanoket, the settlers referred to the Wampanoag as the Pokanoket.

Governor John Carver and Massasoit worked out a peace agreement on March 22, 1621,
making the Pilgrims and Wampanoag allies. According to *Mourt's Relation A Journal of the
Pilgrims at Plymouth*, two of the six agreements read: "That neither he nor any of his should in-
jure or do hurt to any of our people" and "If any did unjustly war against him, we would aid him;
if any did war against us, he should aid us."

This simple treaty was never broken, and the two groups enjoyed a peaceful coexistence.
Massasoit remained an ally of the Pilgrims until his death in 1661. Over time, however, hostilities
grew among new settlers and colonists, and many Indian tribes of the Eastern Woodlands were
devastated, losing lives and land as well as their freedom.

Squanto stayed in Plymouth and taught the new settlers how to fish the rivers, coastline
and sea. He shared the seeds of his ancestors and taught them how to grow corn, beans, pumpkins and squash. He taught them how, where and when to gather various wild plants, fruits,
berries and nuts. In late summer he led them to cranberry bogs to pick the wild berries, which
were new to the Pilgrims, and taught them the patterns of wild game and how to hunt. Through
his native skills, sound advice and loyalty, Squanto saved them from complete devastation. He
also served as a liaison between the Indians and Pilgrims. The settlers learned new skills and
traded with other tribes of the Woodland region as well.

First Sightings

The first explorer to document the wild cranberry may have been Captain John Smith,
the "Admiral of New England," when he voyaged along the coast of the New World in 1614.
According to *John Smith's Works*, "The Herbes and Fruits are of many sorts and kinds: as
Alkermes, currans, mulberries…of certain red berries, called Kermes…and may be yeerly gathered in a good quantity."

Another seventeenth century Englishman, John Josselyn, made two voyages to America, one in 1638 and again in 1663. Returning to England in 1672, he wrote *New Englands Rarities Discovered*, an early, authentic botanical guide to the area's plants and animals. He described the cranberry in detail:

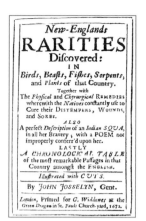

Title page from New Englands Rarities Discovered.

"Cran Berry, or Bear Berry, because Bears use much to feed upon them, is a small, trayling Plant that grows in Salt Marshes, the tender Branches (which are reddish) run out in great length, lying flat on the ground, where at distances they take Root, overspreading sometimes half a score Acres, sometimes in small patches of about a Rood, or the like; the leaves are like Box, but greener, thick and glittering; the Blossoms are very like the Flowers of our English Night Shade, after which succeed the Berries, hanging by long, small stalks no bigger than a hair, at first they are of a pale yellow Colour, afterwards red, and as big as a Cherry, some perfectly Round, others Oval, all of them hollow, or a sower astringent Taste; they are ripe in August and September."

When Roger Williams, pioneer of religious liberty, was forced to flee the Massachusetts Colony, he began living among the Narragansett Indians of southern New England and learned their language. He later founded Rhode Island. Williams, in his famous *Key into the Language of America, An Help to the Language of the Natives of New England,* written in 1643, noted that the Narragansett Indians had a name for cranberries and a high regard for their medicinal purposes. He wrote: "Sasemineash-Another Sharp, Cooling fruit, growing in fresh water in the Winter…; Sweet, like currants, Some Opening, some of a binding nature…." Williams further observed one interesting way the Narragansett used cranberries in their cooking. They took the dried cranberries, sautaash, beat them to a powder and mixed them with parched corn to make sautauthig, "a delicate dish…which is as sweet to them as plum or spice cake to the English."

John Eliot was an early missionary in the region of Concord, Massachusetts. After preaching a sermon in 1647, a question arose asking, "…how it comes to pass that the Sea water was salt, and the Land water fresh." Eliot responded, "Why are Strawberries sweet and Cranberries sowre? There is no reason but the wonderfull worke of God that made them so."

By the late seventeenth century, the American cranberry had gained such popularity that it was considered, along with corn and codfish, one of the most prized foods found in the colonies. In 1677, in order to appease King Charles II over the colony coining its own money, the authorities of the Massachusetts Colony sent him three of their choicest products, a gift comprising "tenn barrells of cranburyes, two hogsheads of special good sampe (Indian corn) and three thousand of cod fish."

16th century (earliest known) woodcut of wild cranberry (European), called marsh wort. — From Henry Lyte: A Nievve Herbal..., *1578.*

In 1686, cranberries were again sent to noted English botanist, John Ray. He, in turn, described the berry and gave it its American name "cranberry." Early evidence of the cranberry's popularity in both New Jersey and Pennsylvania is found in several sources as well: Thomas Budd, a Quaker, settled in Burlington, New Jersey and wrote one of the first books about America. In his little book, *Good Order Established in Pennsylvania and New Jersey in America*, 1685, Budd lists cranberries among the region's natural resources: "Fruits that grow natural in the Countries are Strawberries, Cramberries, Huckleberries, Blackberries, Medlers, Grapes, Plums, Hickory Nuts, Mulberries…."

"Cramberries" is also the term Gabriel Thomas used in *An Historical and Geographical Account of the Province and Country of Pennsylvania and of West-New-Jersey in America,* 1698: "…several sorts of Wild Fruits, as Grapes…Cramberries, and Plumbs, of several sorts…."

Mahlon Stacy, an early settler near Trenton, New Jersey, wrote a letter to his brother in England in 1689: "The cranberries, much like cherries for colour and bigness, which may be kept till fruit come in again…." The settlers obviously learned to store cranberries by observing the Indians. And Stacey enthusiastically endorsed the use of the cranberry in "modern" American cooking: "…an excellent sauce is made of them for venison, turkeys and other great fowl, and they are better to make tarts than either gooseberries or cherries…."

Cranberries were also used as a trade commodity for the Indians in their dealings with the English. According to Stacy, "They (the Indians)…brought to market in season, huckleberries, strawberries, cranberries, grapes and venison. And delivered them as well!…and we have them brought to our homes by the Indians in great plenty." Meanwhile, on the Northwest coast, Lewis and Clark recorded paying "high prices" to a group of Chinook women for "Cramberies."

CRANBERRIES ARE GOOD MEDICINE

Wild cranberries growing along Cape Cod were particularly welcome to the Pilgrims, who had long been deprived of fruit. Their diets consisted almost exclusively of salted meat and biscuits, the same endured by sailors during long voyages. Lacking Vitamin C, many suffered from scurvy. Undoubtedly, they learned of the nutritional and medicinal properties of the cranberry from their Wampanoag friends, who had been using them for hundreds of years. The high Vitamin C content in cranberries provided a natural remedy for scurvy, as John Josseyln noted in 1638: "They are excellent against Scurvey. For the Heat in Feavors. They are also good to allay the fervour of Hot Diseases."

Roger Williams, in *Key into the Language of America* (1643), also noted that "Sasemineash (were) Excellent to conserve against Feavors, of which there are divers kinds…."

Before long, cranberries were being loaded aboard ships embarking on long voyages. It was a staple item for American whaling and clipper ships. In Herman Melville's classic, *Moby-Dick,* a Nantucket seamen parlays the significance of cranberries to the inexperienced Ishmael: "Go out with that crazy Captain Ahab? Never! He flat refused to take cranberries

Yankee soldiers, dining on a Thanksgiving meal of turkey and cranberries, 1864. — Pen and ink by Robert A. Henry, 1989.

aboard. A man could get scurvy, or worse, whaling with the likes of 'im."

In the early and mid-1800s, American medical botanists became interested in indigenous medicines and the cranberry became a popular ingredient in natural remedies. *The American Frugal Housewife* noted: "The Indians have great belief in the efficacy of poultices of stewed cranberries, for the relief of cancers. They apply them fresh and warm every ten or fifteen minutes, night and day." Soon cranberries and cranberry leaves, in various forms and applications, were used in the cure of blood disorders, stomach ailments, liver problems, urinary disorders, diarrhea, diabetes, fevers and other diseases: "They are cooling, slightly laxative, and form an excellent diet both in health and disease...Useful in fevers, diarrhoea, scurvy, dropsy, and many other diseases. Their acid is said to be the oxalic and malic...Their juice mixed with sugar or alcohol keeps a long while, and forms a fine acidulous drink with water allaying thirst, and lessening the heat of the body," wrote Rabinesque in 1830.

Cranberries were probably one of the earliest botanical treatments for cancer and other ailments: "Cancer to cure. Take cranberries, crush them well and apply them to the sore and it will soon be well", wrote Howard Quebec in 1833.

According to Erichsen-Brown, on Delaware Island in 1888, cranberries were used for treating obscure ailments that are unknown to us today: "Cranberries...refrigerant and a fine palliative dressing for acute erysipelas.... The inhabitants make an excellent conserve with the berries which when raw are acidulous and antiscorbutic." Other ailments found cranberries helpful in treatment: "Cranberry branches are steeped as a medicine for pleurisy," wrote Speck in 1915. "A tea for a person who is slightly ill with nausea," wrote H. Smith, in 1932.

A Japanese remedy was recorded in 1925 by Wood and Ruddock: "...cranberries will end a case of piles, cook and eat a fruit dish full two or three times a day.... Cranberries are the best cure for recent erysipelas ever known if applied early. This dangerous malady yields at once. Pound berries and spread on old cotton and apply over entire diseased area and inflammation speedily subsides." (From Constance Crosby, in *Cranberry Harvest*, Spinner Publications, 1989.)

EARLY AMERICAN COOKING WITH CRANBERRIES

Since the settlers had limited ingredients in those first years, familiar recipes from home were modified to incorporate the new fruits and vegetables. In colonial times, food was either boiled, roasted, fried, or baked in a fireplace, and bread was baked in an oven built into the chimney. The women soon learned how adaptable this new fruit was. Mixed with maple sugar, cranberries became a replacement for gooseberries in pies, tarts and sauces and they were turned into thick preserves and sauces that lasted all winter. Many new and imaginative recipes celebrated the cranberry's color, taste, texture, drying and storing qualities.

As the Wampanoag used cranberries in many ways, so did the settlers. John Josselyn, in 1627, noted: "The Indians and English use them much, boyling them with Sugar for Sauce to eat with their Meate, and it is a delicate Sauce, especially for Roast Mutton. Some make tarts with Them as with Goose Berries." Milton Stacey, in 1689, added enthusiastically: "…they are better to make tarts than either gooseberries or cherries."

The first recipe for a cranberry sauce appeared in *The Compleat Cook's Guide,* in 1683 and cranberry juice was created at this time. In 1728, *The Boston News Lette*r included cranberries as one of the staples of an average family diet. *The First American Cookbook,* by Amelia Simmons (1796), found a place for cranberries: "To Stuff and roast a Turkey, or Fowl," the advice was: "… serve up with boiled onions and cramberry-sauce, mangoes, pickles or celery." Cranberries were also listed in the "Tart" section, but the directions were vague: Cramberries. "Stewed, strained and sweetened, put into paste No. 9, and baked gently."

In the early 1800s, the Shakers were flourishing in America, having established eighteen communities of about 6,000 members. Shakers held a strong belief in healthy eating, expressing simplicity and high quality. They were especially noted for their canned goods and preserves, which were stored in crocks, wooden pails, kegs and barrels. They dried cranberries and hung them from the rafters in their cabins. Many cranberry recipes found in the *Shaker Household Journals* include dumplings, puddings, sauces, tarts, cobblers, pies, relishes and even catsup. In 1829, after cranberries were commercially cultivated, *The American Frugal Housewife* was written for "…those who are not ashamed of economy" and included three recipes for cranberries—cranberry pie, cranberry pudding and cranberry jelly.

By this time cranberries were used in households across the country. The ultimate compliment to the cranberry was written in 1830: "Cranberry tarts are one of the American table luxuries." Henry David Thoreau, who used to gather wild cranberries and carry them home to cook, wrote in a journal entry of 1852, "Refreshing, cheering, encouraging…perhaps the prettiest berry…certainly the most novel and interesting."

THE FIRST THANKSGIVING

In England, the Pilgrims' tradition was to celebrate a successful harvest by holding religious observances and feasting. They combined the importance of family, church, prayer, feasting and charity. In the autumn of 1621, they planned to celebrate their good fortune and plentiful harvest with a thanksgiving feast. This celebration came to be known as the First Thanksgiving.

There is much we don't know about that first Thanksgiving in Plymouth, but we do know this: Thanks to the Wampanoag, the Pilgrims had harvested enough food by the fall of 1621 to last through the winter, and their health had improved. In his 1622 book of letters, Edward Winslow wrote: "Our corn did prove well, and God be praised…." They were living comfortably in their homes and had built a church. "I never in my life remember a more seasonable year than we have here enjoyed…I make no question but men might live as contented here as in any part of the world…give God thanks who hath dealt so favorably with us."

Captain Miles Standish, the leader of the Pilgrims, invited Squanto, Samoset, Massasoit and "ninety men" to join in the celebration with 52 Pilgrims. "We have found the Indians very faithful in their covenant of peace with us, very loving and ready to pleasure us. We often go to them, and they come to us…We entertain them familiarly in our houses, and they as friendly bestowing their venison on us."

The Indians included sachems, or council members, from the villages allied with Massasoit, and representatives from each of the Wampanoag villages. For three days the Wampanoag feasted with the Pilgrims, a special time of friendship and camaraderie, though the invitation to the Wampanoag may have been more of a political gesture than an offer of peace and friendship.

Edward Winslow accounts: "Our harvest being gotten in, our governor sent four men on fowling, that so we might after a special manner rejoice together after we had gathered the fruit of our labors. They four in one day killed as much fowl as, with a little help beside, served the company almost a week. At which time, amongst other recreations, we exercised our arms, many of the Indians coming amongst us, and among the rest their greatest, with some ninety men, whom for three days we entertained and feasted, and they went out and killed five deer; which they brought to the plantation and bestowed on our governor; and upon the captain and others. And although it be not always so plentiful as it was at this time with us, yet by the goodness of God, we are so far from want that we often wish you partakers of our Plenty."

Re-enactment of First Thanksgiving, Plimoth Plantation, 1962.

Spinner Collection

The second source documenting the First Thanksgiving is from the book, *Of Plymouth Plantation,* by William Bradford, 1620-1647. "They began now to gather in the small harvest they had, and to fit up their houses and dwelling against winter, being all well recovered in health and strength and had all things in good plenty. For as some were thus employed in affairs abroad, others were exercised in fishing, about cod and bass and other fish, of which they took good store, of which every family had their portion. All the summer there was no want; and now began to come in store of fowl, as winter approached, of which this place did abound when they came first (but afterward decreased by degrees). And besides waterfowl there was great store of wild turkeys, of which they took many, besides venison, etc. Besides, they had about a peck a meal a week to a person, or now since harvest, Indian corn to that proportion. Which made many afterwards write so largely of their plenty here to their friends in England, which were not feigned but true reports."

No specific date is given for the celebration, but it was between September 21, 1621, when the *Shallop* returned from Massachusetts Bay, and November 9, when the *Fortune* arrived with settlers from England.

Today Thanksgiving is a particularly American holiday with a full table of turkey, stuffing, cranberry sauce, pumpkin pie and the enjoyment of friends and family, football and parades. At the start of their Thanksgiving feast, many people take a moment to give thanks for nature's bounty, and for the things in their lives for which they are truly grateful.

"Plymouth in 1622." In this late 19th-century painting, the houses appear a little too large, and the landscape too well-trimmed; but the overall size of the settlement appears accurate.

Painting by W. L. Williams, 1891

THE GUEST LIST

The *Mayflower* passengers celebrating Thanksgiving included sixteen men, four women, twenty-three children and nine hired seamen and servants. Only about half of those who left England in 1620 lived through the first winter. Guests included John Alden, Isaac, Bartholomew, Remember and Mary Allerton, John, Elinor, John Jr. and Francis Billington, William Bradford, William and Mary Brewster and Love and Wrestling Brewster, Peter Browne, Carver's maid-servant, Mary Chilton, Francis and Humility Cooper, John Crackstone, Edward Doley, Francis and Samuel Eaton, Ely, Samuel and Samuel Fuller, Jr., Richard Gardiner, Stephen, Elizabeth, Constance, Giles, Damaris and Oceanus Hopkins, John Howland, William Latham, Edward Lester, Desire Minter, Richard Moore, Priscilla Mullins, Joseph Rogers, Henry Sampson, George Soule, Myles Standish, Elizabeth Tilley, William Trevore, Richard Warren, Resolved and Peregrine White, Edward Winslow, Susanna (White) Winslow, and Gilbert Winslow.

What foods were included in the first Thanksgiving feast? Food included waterfowl—ducks, geese and swans—also wild turkeys, Indian corn and cornmeal, probably in corn bread or corn pudding. Cod, bass and other fish may have included clams, oysters, lobsters, crabs, mussels, scallops, herring, skate, turbot and eels. The Wampanoag brought five deer to the feast.

The meats were most likely roasted or boiled in the traditional English way, and the fish either boiled or grilled in the Indian style. The foods would have been prepared in a simple manner

"The First Thanksgiving." The settlers' first celebration of thanks has been a bit over-dramatized and romanticized by artists and historians.

Painting by Jennie Brownscomb, 1914, in the collection of the Pilgrim Society, Plymouth, MA

Plimoth Plantation Thanksgiving, 1962. — Spinner Collection

Harvest display, Westport, MA Fair. — John K. Robson photograph

in order to feed all of the guests. Many of the wild fruits were no longer in season though some may have been preserved and served. Winslow notes: "Here are grapes, white and red…strawberries, gooseberries, raspas (raspberries)…Plums of three sorts, with black and red."

Walnuts, chestnuts, hickory nuts, and cherries also grew wild in the area. Edible plants picked during the winter might have been served at that table. "Many kinds of herbs we found here in winter, as strawberry leaves…sorrel, yarrow, carvel, brooklime, liverwort, watercresses… leeks and onions…"

The herbs were either boiled along with the meats as "sauce" or used in "sallets," a vegetable dish served raw like a salad or cooked. The first crop of barley survived and provided the colonists with malt for beer. Children drank beer along with the adults. Beans, pumpkins and squash, important crops for both Indians and settlers were probably cooked and served with spices the English brought over with them.

What foods were *not* served at the First Thanksgiving feast? The first planting of English seeds may not have grown abundantly the first year, including carrots, turnips, parsnips, cabbage, onions, radishes, beets, lettuce, skirrets and melons. According to Mr. Winslow, "…our pease not worth the gathering, for we feared they were too late sown. They came up very well, and blossomed, but the sun parched them in the blossom." Sweet potatoes, yams, potatoes, apples and sweet corn were not yet available in early New England. The corn grown by the colonists and Indians was a flint variety, which was good for grinding into cornmeal. Pumpkin pie would not have been served, as sugar was not available. Maple syrup would have been scarce and pie crusts made of flour would not be on the table because of the lack of wheat. Tea and coffee were not used in England or known to the Pilgrims at this time.

Neither Mr. Winslow nor Mr. Bradford mentioned cranberries in their accounts of the first Thanksgiving. However, Mr. Winslow noted there were numerous edible plants "and vines everywhere" growing in Plymouth, some unfamiliar to the English.

THANKSGIVING THROUGH THE YEARS

So how did pumpkin pie, cranberry sauce, and turkey with stuffing become synonymous with Thanksgiving? They most likely came later. The next recorded Thanksgiving was called by Governor Bradford on July 26, 1623, a religious day to give thanks for an end of a drought. On February 22, 1631, settlers of Massachusetts Bay Colony in Boston celebrated the arrival of the ship, Lyon, with a day of prayer and thanksgiving. On September 18, 1639, the governor of Connecticut made a proclamation calling for an annual thanksgiving for "general causes," to thank God for the safety of the colony and the bounty of the season. This became a seasonal custom, though the day was never the same; it came as an announcement by the governor. This custom spread throughout other parts of New England and continued for many years, even though the political picture in New England was changing during the mid-1700s.

Frontispiece from 17th-century English cookbook.

On November 1, 1777, the Continental Congress called for a day of Thanksgiving and all thirteen colonies participated to celebrate the defeat of the British. Other Thanksgivings were called by the Continental Congress in 1778 and 1783 to celebrate political victories and the end of the Revolution. In November of 1789, after much encouragement and debate over the separation of church and state, George Washington, the nation's first president, proclaimed a day of thanksgiving and asked for "All citizens of all religions and all denominations" to celebrate the well-being of the United States.

No days of Thanksgiving were celebrated for eight years when John Adams, who followed Washington, was in office. Thanksgiving returned with President James Madison who called for a national day of prayer and Thanksgiving at the end of the War of 1812. After Madison's term in 1815, Thanksgiving did not receive national recognition, though some individual New England states continued their own Thanksgiving traditions.

In 1846, Sarah Josepha Hale, editor of *Lady's Magazine* and later *Godey's Lady's Book*, petitioned several presidents to make Thanksgiving a national, annual event. In 1863, President Abraham Lincoln called for a day of Thanksgiving to be held on August 6. In response to Ms. Hale's petition, Mr. Lincoln called for a national Thanksgiving Day to be held on the last Thursday in November and Thanksgiving became a national event.

A Holiday Cranberry Tradition

By the mid-1800's American cranberries were being shipped overseas, where recipes using cranberries appeared in English cookbooks. Cranberries had become a distinctively American fruit and new hallmark of American cuisine. By the 1880s, cranberries were shipped in 100-pound barrels, packed in water, and sold in New York, Philadelphia and

100-lb. barrels at Bailey's screenhouse are ready to be shipped, South Carver, circa 1900. — Courtesy of Nancy Davison.

Chicago. Thanksgiving was becoming a more secular holiday as the focus shifted to friends, family, football and, of course, the feast. As immigrants poured in from Europe through the early 1890s, they encountered a great deal of pressure to assimilate. They easily adopted Thanksgiving, that pure American holiday, as it also represented freedom and success in a new land.

When Gimbel's Department Store in Philadelphia held the first Thanksgiving Parade in 1921, other cities followed. Whole, fresh cranberries could now be shipped across the country during the holiday season. Canned cranberry sauce was a new seasonal favorite, too. In the 1930s fresh cranberries were sold in cellophane packages. Free booklets and recipe cards gave homemakers an idea of the many things they could do with cranberries. At this time, Ocean Spray began marketing a cranberry juice cocktail—a new concept. Meanwhile, cranberries were catching on and cooks across the country started making their own sauce, relish, jelly, sherbet, pies and puddings for Thanksgiving. The uniquely American Thanksgiving menu became synonymous with the holiday—turkey with stuffing and cranberry sauce.

To boost the economy and lengthen the shopping season, in 1939, President Franklin D. Roosevelt changed Thanksgiving Day to the third Thursday in November. In 1941, Congress made Thanksgiving a legal national holiday and changed it back to the fourth Thursday. In 1943-

Juice cocktail, 1940.

A.D. Makepeace Company workers loading a shipment of berries at Tremont, 1920s.

Ocean Spray Cranberries

A. D. Makepeace Co. photograph

1944, most of the entire United States cranberry crop was purchased by the federal government and sent oversees to servicemen and women in dehydrated and evaporated form, so few were found on Thanksgiving tables. In 1946, when Ocean Spray introduced bagged fresh whole berries, cranberries were once again on the Thanksgiving menu.

In November 1959, the entire cranberry crop suffered from a catastrophe. Aminotriazole, a toxic weed killer, had been used on some cranberry crops in Washington and Oregon. Even though a very small percentage of the cranberries had been contaminated, approximately 79 percent of all canned cranberries and 63 percent of fresh berries were destroyed on November 9 of that year. Hence, few Americans celebrated Thanksgiving with cranberries that year.

Today, Thanksgiving is still celebrated on the fourth Thursday in November, and for most Americans, the traditional menu of turkey, stuffing, cranberry sauce and pumpkin pie has remained unchanged.

CAPE COD BOGS

In Massachusetts, cranberries growing wild on public land were available to all. However, as their popularity grew and demand increased, many towns passed laws to reserve the cranberry harvest for townspeople and local tribes. Soon after, as common lands became privately owned, wild cranberries became scarce. Outsiders who came to pick were a problem and fines were established for those caught picking unripe berries before the designated day of the harvest. In the early nineteenth century, as demand for wild cranberries grew and the natural supply was insufficient for the growing population, the idea of cranberry cultivation took root.

Several innovators took an interest in commercial cultivation. Henry Hall, a Revolutionary War veteran and sea captain from the Cape Cod town of Dennis, became the first commercial grower. Observing that wild cranberries grew better when beach sand blew over them, Hall began transplanting the vines, fencing them in for protection and covering them with sand. His method was so successful that by 1820, he was shipping cranberries to Boston and New York City. Knowledge of his techniques quickly spread, and so did the cranberry industry. Many landowners elsewhere on Cape Cod turned marsh lands and meadows into bogs, and Cape Cod became the birthplace of the cranberry industry.

In 1846, Captain Alvin Cahoon, who had seen Hall's vines, planted his own bog in the Pleasant Lake area of Harwich. His cousin and neighbor, Captain Cyrus Cahoon, also began developing bogs and together the two men experimented and developed methods of cultivation that gave a foundation to the young industry. Within ten years, the total cranberry land on Cape Cod was 1074 acres, with Harwich the leader.

The Makepeace name is well-known in the industry today. In 1854, Abel D. Makepeace bought land in Hyannis for farming, caught cranberry fever and built a small bog. At first he was unsuccessful but he persisted and a decade later his bog was producing over 2,000 barrels of cranberries. Within the next few years, he formed a company and built

Handpicking on a Carver bog, circa 1890.
— Ocean Spray Cranberries photograph.

bogs in Barnstable, Plymouth and Carver. Others followed suit. It now became clear that a forum was needed for the exchange of ideas and information on cranberry cultivation and marketing. The Cape Cod Cranberry Growers' Association was formed in 1888 with Makepeace the founding member. Makepeace was an inventor, improving the snap scoop, picking devices and mechanical separators. Though he was a tough businessman, he was also known as a fair employer. (From Christy Lowrance, in *Cranberry Harvest*, Spinner Publications, 1989.)

The Finns and The Cape Verdeans

The swampy woodlands of Cape Cod may have reminded immigrant Finns of Swomi, the Finnish word for swamp, and many eventually settled here out of nostalgia for the land they left behind. When Makepeace built the "Big Bog" at Wankinco and Frogfoot in the mid-1880s, his

Finnish workers provided the labor to build and maintain these projects—weeding and ditching as well as picking and sorting. As the news spread, more Finnish workers arrived to work on bogs in Wareham, Carver, Middleboro, Barnstable and Sandwich.

Finnish families working the bogs in
South Carver, MA, circa 1920. — Courtesy of Mary Korpinen.

Hard work paid off for the Finns as they were in demand to fill positions as foremen and supervisors. By the 1920s, enough Finnish families had settled in connected areas of Middleboro, Carver and Wareham to establish an active community. Several hundred bog owners were listed in Massachusetts in 1934 and 70 were Finnish, most of whom owned bogs of ten acres or less.

Today the Finns are considered to have a knack for cranberry growing, creating many of the inventions that achieved wide use in the industry. The Mathewson picker was developed in 1923 by a Finn, Oscar Tervo; the snap scoop was refined by Kataja, and Everett Niemi developed a method for making and packing dehydrated cranberries during the war. Thanks to their fortitude and strong desire to work the land, many third and fourth generation Finns are growing cranberries. (From Linda Donaghy, in *Cranberry Harvest,* Spinner Publications, 1989.)

The Cape Verde Islands off the west coast of Africa have a long-suffering history of drought and Portuguese colonial rule, and many islanders looked for opportunity elsewhere. The earliest emigrants to America joined the crews of whaling ships in anchor there to pick up supplies. By 1900, a pressing need for cheap labor in both the expanding textile mills and the cranberry industry of southeastern New England, led to a steady influx of Cape Verdean immigrants.

Cape Verdeans were known as rugged farmers and they brought a robust aptitude and passion for the land to their work on the bogs. Yet few Cape Verdeans became owners; instead they remained migrant laborers, residing off-season primarily in Wareham and New Bedford, Massachusetts and Providence, Rhode Island. The work was hard, the pay low, and women and children were part of the migrant labor force. Nevertheless, many old timers recall pleasant memories of bonfires and story-telling, dewy mornings and record-breaking scooping. The more fortunate men found year-round employment on the bogs.

As the Cape Verdeans began to settle in Plymouth County and on Cape Cod, they encountered increasing prejudice in traditional Yankee strongholds, given their unmistakable African as well as Portuguese roots. But the Cape Verdeans were valuable laborers and they helped the cranberry industry thrive in Southeastern Massachusetts. (From Marilyn Halter, in *Cranberry Harvest,* Spinner Publications, 1989.)

"Fanny Bento. Said 9 years old. Was picking with her father on a private bog near Bang's Bog," Rochester, MA, 1911. — Lewis Hine photograph.

Cape Verdean family, Wareham, MA, 1950s. — Spinner Collection.

THE JERSEY PINES

The English settlers in New Jersey were well acquainted with the cranberry and in 1789, the state legislature passed a law protecting the wild, ripening fruit. In the 1850s and 1860s, three of New Jersey's major growers started their bogs: Joseph C. Hinchsman, Daniel H. Shreve and Theodore Budd.

Sorting cranberries.
— From White: Cranberry Culture, *1870.*

John "Peg-Leg" Webb of Ocean County was probably New Jersey's best-known early grower. (As a boy, he lost a leg to a falling tree.) Webb, a true experimenter, was the first in New Jersey to discover the benefits of covering the bog muck with sand before planting. He stored his berries on the second floor of his barn and, because of his wooden leg, retrieved them by pouring them down the stairs. One day he noticed that the sound berries bounced down to the bottom while the poor ones stayed on the steps. The "bounce principle" has been used ever since in various cranberry sorting processes.

By 1870, New Jersey moved ahead of Massachusetts as the nation's largest producer of berries, but Jerseyites paid less attention to sound bog building and soon fell behind again. Forming the American Cranberry Growers' Association in 1873, they began marketing their crop at Charles Wilkinson's produce house in Philadelphia, which soon overtook Boston and New York as the leading cranberry market.

One of the largest cranberry bogs in the country was Whitesbog, which had its own post office, general store, housing compound and power plant. Elizabeth White ran the bog and made a name for herself advancing cranberry and blueberry cultivation. Today, Jersey growers produce about 10 percent of the crop, chiefly in Ocean, Burlington and Atlantic counties, which make up New Jersey's "Pine Barrens," similar to the Cape Cod and Plymouth growing regions.

Young New Jersey picker, 1911. — Lewis Hine photograph.

Library of Congress

Early water harvesting machines in New Jersey, 1962.

USDA Soil Conservation Service

THE WISCONSIN MARSHES

As early as 1700, Native Americans gathered what they called "atoqua," or cranberries, which they and the settlers harvested for their own use. The berries grew in the marshlands and early growers fenced off naturally occurring vines for cultivation. The marshes held bogs of soil surrounded by muck and covered with grasses or small brush. Growers soon found that ditching and draining these bogs increased production.

"Taking floaters" on a Wisconsin bog, 1930s. Wisconsin growers are credited with being the first to develop water harvesting techniques.

The state's first large-scale grower was Edward Sackett of Aurora, in the 1860s. Berlin County was the early focus of cranberry growing in Wisconsin, but it gradually gave way to the swamplands of glacial Lake Wisconsin in the central part of the state. Today it is centered in Wood, Jackson and Juneau Counties in northwestern and north-central Wisconsin.

By 1905, water harvesting became popular in Wisconsin. One of the first growers to harvest on the flood was Andrew Searles, who cultivated native vines and developed the Searles berry variety that now makes up 65 percent of the Wisconsin crop. Wisconsin surpassed Massachusetts in annual production and in the late 1980s and currently produces about 52 percent of the annual crop (see chart on page 35).

THE PACIFIC PLANTATIONS

In 1874, Charles Dexter McFarlin built one of the finest bogs in Carver, Massachusetts but when a frost wiped out his first crop, he decided to return to the west coast where he and two brothers had traveled during the Gold Rush Days. His father had always gathered the wild native berries that grew in Carver's "New Meadows," and his brother, Thomas, had de-

Hauling vine cuttings for a new bog in the Washington wilderness, circa 1900. — Ocean Spray Cranberries photograph.

veloped the McFarlin variety. Charles settled in what is now Coos County, Oregon, an area that reminded him of his hometown, and he sent back to Carver for McFarlin vines. Thus, Oregon's cranberry industry was launched.

In Washington, Anthony Chabot, a French Canadian, bought some sparsely inhabited land near Long Beach in Pacific County and built the state's first bog in 1881. Later, Ed Benn built the first bog in the Grayland area in 1912 and soon sold tracts of land to Finnish settlers who became a large part of Washington's cranberry industry. The McFarlin is the predominant variety grown in Washington and Oregon. The two states combined produce about seven percent of the national cranberry crop. (From Robert Demanche, in *Cranberry Harvest*, Spinner Publications, 1989.)

PRODUCTION FIGURES FOR UNITED STATES IN 2001			
STATE	ACREAGE	BARRELS (100 LBS./BB.)	PERCENT OF U.S.
Massachusetts	13,900	1,416,000	29.6
Wisconsin	15,100	2,840,000	51.6
New Jersey	3,700	566,000	8.6
Oregon	2,400	365,000	7.4
Washington	1,500	142,000	2.8
TOTAL U.S.	36,600	5,329,000	100

Source: USDA, National Agricultural Statistics, 2002

GROWING AN INDUSTRY

Cranberries were mostly handpicked until the 1850s, when pickers started using wooden scoops to comb through the vines and lift off the berries. Mechanical harvesting did not begin until the 1950s. Today dry and wet harvesting are the preferred methods; in dry harvesting, growers use a mechanical picker that looks like a giant lawn mower. The picker combs the berries off the vine with moving metal teeth; a conveyor belt carries them to a box at the back of the machine, then they are poured in large containers and air-lifted by helicopter to waiting trucks. Cranberries harvested by the dry method supply the "fresh-fruit" market (and those most often used in baking and cooking), as wet-harvested berries contain too many bruised and softened berries.

In wet harvesting, the preferred method since the 1960s, mechanical water reels are guided through the bogs, which have been flooded to a depth of six to eighteen inches. The water reels, nicknamed "egg beaters," stir up the water with sufficient force to dislodge the ripe berries from their vines. The berries, which have four interior compartments that fill with air, then float to the surface. Harvesters corral the floating berries to waiting trucks using mechanical elevators or berry pumps. Most wet-harvested cranberries are frozen and used primarily for processed foods, juices, sauces and relishes. More than eighty-five percent of the cranberry crop is wet-harvested.

All harvested cranberries are transported to a central receiving station where they undergo a thorough sorting process. Good firm cranberries have pockets of air inside them that make them good bouncers. If a cranberry is damaged or spoiled, it will not bounce. A machine called a separator, dating back to the late 1800s, utilizes the natural bouncing quality of a good cranberry.

Each berry has several chances to bounce over a wooden barrier and must bounce seven times. If the berry is bruised, soft or rotten, it will not bounce, and it falls into a disposal bin. The good berries are then inspected for color, weight, and skin texture.

Cranberry bogs are flooded from late December through mid-March to protect the vines from winter injury. A layer of sand is applied to the cranberry bog every few years, which helps to stimulate growth, improve drainage and control weeds and insects. Brush and trees around the perimeter of the bog are also removed at this time. Around mid-March, growers drain the winter flood, the vines slowly come out of dormancy and the growing season begins. The buds are watered through a sprinkler system to protect them during the evening or early morning.

In the spring, the bogs are covered with pink blossoms and beehives are brought in from early June through mid July to pollinate the flower. In summer, cranberries require up to one inch of water per week and if the rainfall is inadequate, the plants are watered through a sprinkler system. Harvesting occurs between mid-September and early November.

Cranberry production supports an extensive wetlands system that is vital to the protection of many varieties of plants, animals and waterfowl. Cranberry growers help preserve wetlands, providing safe and natural habitats where plant and animal life will flourish. Cranberry bogs provide a diverse and safe breeding, feeding and wintering habitat for a variety of birds and animals. Many endangered plant species thrive in cranberry wetlands.

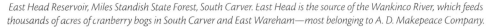

East Head Reservoir, Miles Standish State Forest, South Carver. East Head is the source of the Wankinco River, which feeds thousands of acres of cranberry bogs in South Carver and East Wareham—most belonging to A. D. Makepeace Company.

John K. Robson photograph

Cranberry agriculture is a compatible and environmentally sound use of open space. The practices and systems employed by cranberry growers protect and preserve wetlands. They have developed a sophisticated water management system to conserve water by recycling water from bog to bog and grower to grower, filtering groundwater and providing flood control. The cranberry's growth cycle and harvest requires the support of a large complex ecological system that includes wetlands, uplands, rivers, streams, ponds and reservoirs. In turn, cranberries thrive in the presence of a unique combination of sandy soil, a favorable climate and underlying geological conditions that help maintain a sufficient supply of water.

Cranberry growers responsibly manage natural resources, as it is critical to the survival and proliferation of their product to make sure the wetlands are clean and undisturbed. On average, every planted acre is supported by 4-10 acres of surrounding land. These woodlands and wetlands provide open-space, wildlife habitat, groundwater recharge and a buffer to suburban sprawl.

Fewer than one thousand cranberry growers operate in Oregon, Washington, Wisconsin, Massachusetts, New Jersey, British Columbia and Quebec. Smaller acreages flourish in Michigan, Minnesota, New York, Maine, Ontario, Nova Scotia, Prince Edward Island, and New Brunswick. Cranberries are now grown commercially in Chile.

A springtime greening-up on A. D. Makepeace Company's Big Bog along the Wankinco watershed in East Wareham, MA.

John K. Robson photograph

MEDICINAL AND HEALTH BENEFITS

The medicinal values attributed to cranberries hundreds of years ago by both the Indians of the Eastern Woodlands and earliest settlers have been validated by researchers around the world. What was once medicinal folklore is now scientifically based fact. Since 1984, studies have shown that cranberries have numerous health benefits, particularly their "anti-adhesion" effect on certain bacteria. With increasing interest in alternative medicine, natural ingredients and overall health, cranberries are turning up in more recipes and packaged foods and have become a staple in many American homes.

Health researchers are proving that cranberries are a healthy, low calorie fruit that can help fight bacteria naturally, particularly in the urinary tract. Also, evidence suggests that cranberries inhibit certain bacteria in the stomach and oral cavity. Research on the potential benefits of cranberries on heart disease and cancer prevention is ongoing.

Chemically, the cranberry consists of water, plant fibers, sugar, acids, pectin, waxy materials, protein, calcium, magnesium, potassium and phosphorus, plus various vitamins. Cranberry juice contains proanthocyanidins, or condensed tannins, which actually "disable" certain harmful bacteria that cause infection. With just 25 calories per half cup, raw cranberries contain essentially no fat and no cholesterol, are low in sodium, high in fiber and Vitamin C.

NUTRITIONAL VALUE OF CRANBERRIES PER CUP		
	Raw (1 cup = 113 gm)	Sauce (1 cup = 227gm) sweetened, canned, cooked
Calories	54.0	549
Protein	0.5 gm	0.3 gm
Fat	0.8 gm	0.8 gm
Carbohydrates	12.8 gm	142.4 gm
Calcium	16 mg	22 mg
Phosphorus	12 mg	19 mg
Iron	0.7 mg	0.8 mg
Vitamin A Value (I.U.)	50	80
Vitamin B1 Thiamine	0.03 mg	0.06 mg
Vitamin B2 Riboflavin	0.02 mg	0.06 mg
Vitamin B2 Complex Niacin	0.1 mg	0.3 mg
Niacin	0.1 mg	0.3 mg
Vitamin C Ascorbic Acid	13 mg	5 mg

SOURCE: WWW.CRANBERRYLINK.COM

Although the medical community has long believed that cranberry juice decreased the risk and helped alleviate the symptoms of urinary tract infections, scientific evidence was lacking. In a breakthrough study in 1998, a research team from Rutgers isolated compounds called condensed tannins or proanthocyanidins from cranberry fruit. They were found to have anti-adhesion properties, and thus are able to prevent Escherichia coli (E. coli) bacteria—the primary bacteria responsible for urinary tract infections—from attaching to cells in the urinary tract.

Cranberries also contain plant chemicals that may play a role in preventing certain types of cancer. Epidemiological evidence has long supported the role of naturally occurring anti-cancer and protective heart agents in fruits and vegetables. These plant chemicals are called flavonoids and include anthocyanins (which gives the cranberry its color), proanthocyanidins and flavonols.

Cranberries are also a rich source of the flavonoid, quercetin, which inhibits breast and colon cancers. The extract contains antioxidants, which play a fundamental role in slowing the oxidation that leads to heart disease. The cranberry has the ability to inhibit oxidation of LDL cholesterol, so it may help in maintaining cardiovascular health. Researchers have also connected the cranberry with healthy gums. The same "anti-adhesion" properties that prevent bacteria from forming in the urinary tract prevent bacteria from forming in the mouth. This "bacteria inhibiting" effect minimizes the formation of dental plaque, a leading cause of gum disease.

The good news goes on. Compounds found in cranberries may have a role in protecting against ulcer-causing bacteria. Cranberry compounds, identified as condensed tannis or proanthocyanidins, stop certain disease causing bacteria from sticking to the stomach lining.

Susan Mann of Plymouth corrals berries at her family's Garland bog, 1989. These berries are a large, red and white variety called Stevens, which were first cultivated in Wisconsin. They have a high yield and, if harvested late, turn a deep red.

Joseph D. Thomas photograph

BUYING CRANBERRIES

You can buy fresh cranberries in the market from mid-September through December. Fresh cranberries will keep well in the refrigerator up to four weeks in an unopened bag. Before using fresh berries, rinse them under cold water and discard any soft, bruised or discolored berries. Because the cranberry season is short, stock up on fresh berries, which can be frozen up to a year. Freeze them right in their packaging without washing them first. Before using, rinse and discard any bruised or discolored berries. They do not need to be thawed before using them in recipes.

When cooking cranberries, boil them until the skins crack in order to allow the sugar to penetrate the fruit. One 12-ounce bag yields approximately 3 cups of whole cranberries. One pound (16 ounces) of whole cranberries yields about 4 cups of cranberries. And 2 cups of whole berries yields 2 cups of chopped cranberries.

Dried cranberries are slightly tart, delicious as a snack, perfect in recipes calling for dried fruit, and a treat when added to salads and other dishes. Dried cranberries can be used in many of the recipes in this book calling for fresh, frozen whole or chopped cranberries. Simply remember to reduce the amount of sugar being called for in the recipe, since the dried cranberries have already been sweetened during their processing.

Corralled berries are raked into a conveyer or "elevator" that carries then deposits the berries into an 18 wheeler on the "shore."

Gathering dry-harvested berries via "bog buggy," on the Decas Brothers' Stuart Bog, Rochester, MA.

Joseph D. Thomas photograph

Joseph D. Thomas photograph

Chapter One

....

Relishes, Sauces, Conserves, Preserves, Syrups, Jams and Glazes

Simple Cranberry Sauce

Gold leaf engraving on the cloth cover of Eastman: The Cranberry and its Culture, *1856.*

There are many delicious cranberry variations to be discovered. Conserves, preserves and sauces all start with fruit, sugar and liquid and require a short period of cooking. They can be stored in sterilized jars and sealed or enjoyed within a couple weeks. Just as the Native Americans, new settlers and Shakers utilized ingredients seasonally available to them, you can add to cranberries any fruits available fresh or frozen throughout the year. Add more sugar to taste if you prefer a sweeter sauce.

BASIC INSTRUCTIONS:

Combine selected fruit and cranberries and place in a large saucepan. Add sugar to taste, usually 1–1½ cups for every 12-ounce bag of cranberries (about 3 cups) or 2 cups for every pound of cranberries (about 4 cups). Add liquid such as water or fruit juice (between ½ to ¾ cup liquid for every 3 cups of fruit). Bring to a boil and simmer for 15 minutes or until liquid has reduced and the fruit has thickened. Cool completely before using or storing.

Store sauces in the refrigerator in tightly sealed jars or containers for up to two weeks. The sauces can also be frozen.

Traditional Cranberry Sauce

MAKES ABOUT 2½ CUPS

¾ cup water

1½ cups sugar

One 12-ounce bag of fresh or frozen cranberries (about 3 cups)

This recipe has been written in various forms since the 1930s. It was originally called "Ten-Minute" Cranberry Sauce by the Eatmor Cranberry Company. It hasn't changed a bit, except now it can be made easily in the microwave oven, as well.

Put all ingredients into a 2 quart pan. Boil gently for about ten minutes, or until all the cranberries have popped open. The sauce will be a little watery. Cool. Sauce will thicken as it cools. For one pound of cranberries, use 1¼ cups water and 2 cups sugar (sweeten to taste).

MICROWAVE INSTRUCTIONS:

In a glass or microwave safe bowl, put in all the ingredients. Cover with plastic wrap. Cook on HIGH for 4 minutes. Stir. Cook on HIGH for 3 minutes. Stir. If the cranberries have not all popped open, continue to cook for another minute or two. Cool. Sauce will thicken as it cools.

Add more sugar to taste if you prefer a sweeter sauce.

Cranberry Orange Sauce

MAKES ABOUT 2½ CUPS

This is a delicious version of the traditional "Ten Minute" Cranberry Sauce. from the 1930s. It still takes only ten minutes to cook!

In a medium saucepan, combine all the ingredients. Boil gently, and cook for 10 minutes or until all the cranberries have popped open. Cool. Remove cinnamon stick. Serve at room temperature.

MICROWAVE DIRECTIONS:
Place all ingredients in a microwave safe bowl. Reduce water to ⅛ cup. Cover tightly with plastic wrap. Cook on HIGH 4 minutes. Stir. Cook for 4 more minutes on HIGH or until the cranberries have popped open. Let sit to cool and thicken.

One 12-ounce bag fresh or
 frozen cranberries
1 cup sugar
Juice of 1 orange or fresh orange
 juice measuring ½ cup
Grated rind of one orange
1 stick cinnamon
¼ cup water

Cranberry Raspberry Sauce

MAKES ABOUT 2½ CUPS

Place the cranberries and water in a medium sauce pan or pot.

Stir in the sugar and cook on medium heat for 5-10 minutes or until the cranberries have almost all popped open. Add the raspberries and continue to cook for about 5 more minutes or until the sauce is well blended.

Delicious served over *Grilled Chicken Breasts with Caramelized Walnuts*, over johnnycakes or flapjacks or with *Cranberry Orange Scones*. Serve warm or chilled. Keeps in the refrigerator up to two weeks.

3 cups cranberries
 (12-ounce bag)
1 cup water
1½ cups sugar
1 12-ounce bag frozen
 raspberries

Cranberry Lemon Sauce

This sauce is very tangy and delicious!

Add the grated rind from 2 lemons and 2 tablespoons fresh lemon juice to the *Traditional Cranberry Sauce* recipe *(page 42)*. Increase the sugar to 2 cups or to taste. Cook as directed.

*An engraving of the Bell cranberry variety, 1856.
— From Eastwood: Cranberry…Culture.*

*John Josselyn, an
Englishman visiting New England in
1638 and again in 1663,
wrote in detail of the animals and
plants which he found in "the new
land." He wrote, "...The Indians and
English use them (cranberries) much,
boyling them with Sugar for
Sauce to eat with their Meate, and it
is a delicate Sauce, especially for
Roast Mutton."*

Cranberry Walnut Sauce

Add 1 cup coarsely chopped walnuts and grated rind from one orange to the *Traditional Cranberry Sauce (page 42)* when it has finished cooking.

Spiced Cranberry Sauce

Add ½ teaspoon ground cinnamon, ¼ teaspoon ground clove, ¼ teaspoon ground ginger and ¼ teaspoon ground allspice to the *Cranberry Orange Sauce* recipe *(page 43)*. Cook as directed.

Cranberry Orange Raisin Conserve

Add 1 cup raisins to the *Cranberry Orange Sauce (page 43)* recipe when the sauce has finished cooking.

Cranberry Orange Raisin Walnut Conserve

Add 1 cup chopped walnuts to *Cranberry Orange Raisin Conserve (page 43)*.

*An early jar of cranberry sauce, 1930s.
Ocean Spray's success throughout the 30s,
40s and 50s was a direct result of clever
merchandising and advertising.*

Ocean Spray Cranberries photograph

Cranberry Pear Preserves

Add 2 fresh pears, peeled, cored and diced to the *Cranberry Orange Sauce* recipe. Cook as directed.

Cranberry Persimmon Sauce

Add 2 ripe persimmons, peeled and cubed to the *Cranberry Orange Sauce* recipe. Increase sugar to 1½ cups. Add ⅛ teaspoon ground cloves. Combine all ingredients and cook as directed.

Cranberry Persimmon Mango Preserves

Add 1 cup frozen mango chunks to the *Cranberry Persimmon Sauce* recipe. Cook as directed.

Gingered Cranberry Sauce with Almonds

MAKES ABOUT 3 CUPS

Combine the cranberries, sugar, orange juice, water, ginger and orange rind in a medium saucepan. Cook over medium heat until the cranberries have all popped open, approximately 10 minutes. Remove from the heat. Stir in the almonds. Serve chilled.

— *Marilyn Pollak Scheffler, Villa Park, CA*

One 12-ounce bag cranberries
2 cups sugar
½ cup orange juice
¼ cup water
¼ cup finely chopped candied ginger
2 tablespoons finely grated orange rind
½ cup toasted slivered almonds

Cranberry Port Sauce with Thyme

MAKES ABOUT 2¾ CUPS
ENOUGH TO ACCOMPANY A LARGE BIRD, OR 10 SERVINGS.

This sauce is delicious served with goose, pheasant or other game or poultry. Prepare the bird by pan frying, grilling or roasting. If pan frying or roasting, skim the fat from the pan and use the pan juices as part of the sauce. Use prepared chicken or veal stock or a stock made with the giblets of the bird. If making a giblet stock, reduce and strain the stock through a sieve before using it in the sauce.

In the sauté pan used for pan frying, or in a clean 2-quart sauté pan if roasting or grilling, heat the broth or stock over medium heat and bring to a simmer. Add the cranberries and sugar, and continue to cook 10-15 minutes until the berries have popped and the sauce has begun to thicken. Add any other pan juices that may have accumulated during cooking. Add the port and thyme, and bring back to a simmer. Continue to cook for a few more minutes. Turn the heat off. The sauce will thicken as it cools. If the sauce becomes too thick, add more broth or more port.

1 cup chicken broth, homemade stock or pan juices drained of fat
3 cups fresh or frozen cranberries
1 cup sugar
½ cup Port
2 teaspoons chopped fresh thyme
Sprigs of fresh thyme for garnish

Corralled cranberries on a Decas Brothers cranberry bog in South Carver, MA

Mango Lime Cranberry Conserve

Add 2 cups frozen diced mango chunks, 1 tablespoon lime juice, the grated rind from 1 lime and ¼ cup more sugar to the *Traditional Cranberry Sauce* recipe (page 42). Cook as directed.

Joseph D. Thomas photograph

Fresh Cranberry Orange Relish

MAKES 3½ CUPS

1 orange, quartered and
    seeded
4 cups fresh cranberries
1½ cups sugar
2 tablespoons Cointreau or
    Grand Marnier liqueur

Cranberry Orange Relish
(photo page 68)

My daughter, Dana, made this fresh relish at her pre-school in a food grinder. It's that easy! I added the liqueur! The food processor speeds the process.

In a food processor, put the metal blade in place. Put the orange slices in and process until coarsely chopped. Transfer to a bowl. With the metal blade in place, add the cranberries. Process until finely chopped. Return the orange to the processor. Add the sugar and liqueur. Process to mix. Store in the refrigerator.

Fresh Cranberry Relish

There are many delicious cranberry-fruit relish combinations. Relishes are not cooked. The cranberries and other fruits are chopped in a food processor, food grinder or by hand. They are combined with sugar and sometimes nuts. The relishes are stored in the refrigerator and will generally keep for 3 days or so.

Apple, Pecan & Orange Cranberry Relish

MAKES ABOUT 5½ CUPS

2 Granny Smith apples, peeled,
    cored and coarsely chopped
1 cup chopped pecans, roasted

Combine all ingredients with the *Fresh Cranberry Orange Relish* recipe. Prepare as directed.

Mango Cranberry Orange Relish

MAKES ABOUT 5 CUPS

Add 2 mangoes, peeled and diced to the *Fresh Cranberry Orange Relish*. Combine all ingredients. The liqueur can be omitted. Prepare as directed.

Shaker Cranberry Orange Relish

MAKES ABOUT 5 CUPS

If you strung all the cranberries produced in North America this year, they would wrap around the earth about forty-five times!

Add 1 Granny Smith apple, cored and coarsely chopped and 1 cup finely chopped fresh or canned pineapple to the *Fresh Cranberry Orange Relish*. Combine all ingredients. The liqueur can be omitted. Prepare as directed.

Cranberry Salsa

MAKES APPROXIMATELY 2 CUPS

Place the cranberries in a food processor. Pulse a few times until the cranberries are chopped. Add all the other ingredients. Process just until everything is well mixed. Pour into a serving bowl. Cover and refrigerate until ready to serve. The taste improves if allowed to sit for a few hours or overnight.

You can add fresh mango, pineapple, or other fruits to this basic salsa. Add more cilantro, onion, lemon juice or sugar to taste.

2 cups whole cranberries
1 fresh jalapeño pepper, seeded and minced
½ cup red pepper, finely diced
¼ cup fresh cilantro, chopped
½ cup red onion, finely diced
¼ cup fresh Italian flat leaf parsley, chopped
½ cup celery, finely diced
2 tablespoons lemon juice
1 tablespoon sugar
⅛ teaspoon salt

Cranberry Catsup

MAKES 3 CUPS

This catsup looks, smells and tastes like traditional tomato catsup. It is easy to make and makes a great holiday gift to be enjoyed all year.

In a medium sauce pan bring the cranberries, water and shallots to a boil. Lower the heat and simmer for about 15 minutes. Cool 10 minutes. Pour the mixture into a food processor or blender. Puree. In a cheesecloth spice bag or cheesecloth square secured with string, place the cloves, allspice, peppercorns and cinnamon stick. Return the cranberries to the sauce pan. Add the vinegar, sugar, salt and spice bag. Simmer for about 30 minutes, stirring frequently, until the mixture has thickened. Cool slightly and remove the spice bag. Ladle the catsup into sterilized jars. Seal. Store in a dark cupboard or in the refrigerator.

1 pound fresh or frozen cranberries
¾ cup water
2 large shallots, minced (about ⅔ cup)
1 teaspoon whole cloves
1 teaspoon whole allspice
½ teaspoon whole black peppercorns
1 large whole cinnamon stick
½ cup apple cider vinegar
1¼ cup sugar
1½ teaspoons salt

Cranberry Mustard

MAKES ¾ CUP • RECIPE CAN BE DOUBLED

This easy-to-prepare mustard is colorful and tangy — a nice accompaniment to sliced turkey or ham.

Combine all the ingredients and stir well. If you do not have any homemade cranberry sauce available, use whole berry canned cranberry sauce. You can add more brown sugar, honey and lemon juice to taste.

⅓ cup Dijon-style prepared mustard
¼ cup homemade cranberry sauce
1 teaspoon honey
1 teaspoon brown sugar
½ teaspoon fresh lemon juice
¼ teaspoon ginger

Cranberry Maple Syrup

SERVES 4 · MAKES 1½ CUPS

1 cup pure maple syrup
1 cup fresh or frozen whole
  cranberries

Simmer the maple syrup with the cranberries for 5 minutes in a one quart sauce pan until the cranberries have just burst. Remove from heat. Serve over flapjacks, waffles or French toast.

Cranberry Maple Brown Sugar Syrup

MAKES 2¼ CUPS · SERVES 6-8

½ cup water
½ cup brown sugar
1 cup whole fresh or frozen
  cranberries
1 cup pure maple syrup

Place the water, brown sugar and cranberries in a one quart sauce pan. Boil for 5 minutes until the cranberries just pop open and the sauce begins to thicken. Add the maple syrup. Stir and bring to a boil. Turn off the heat and keep warm until ready to serve.

Spiced Cranberry Glaze

⅔ cup cranberry juice
½ cup orange or tangerine
  marmalade

This simple glaze has two versions. Try them both!

Put the juice and marmalade in a glass measuring cup or bowl. Microwave, uncovered, for 1 minute on HIGH. Stir.

FOR POULTRY:
Add ½ teaspoon paprika and ½ teaspoon ground cinnamon

FOR HAM :
Add ½ teaspoon ground cinnamon and ½ teaspoon nutmeg

Glaze before cooking and continue to baste with glaze during cooking.

Inside Ocean Spray's processing plant in Hanson, MA, 1912. The cranberry sauce was prepared manually and hand-filled and hand-sealed in #10 cans.

Ocean Spray Cranberries photograph

Cranberry Butter

SERVES 15

This butter is delicious spread on hot rolls, biscuits, muffins or scones.

In a food processor, mixing bowl or by hand, combine all the ingredients until they are well blended. Place the cranberry butter on a piece of plastic wrap and form into a log. Squeeze out, or blot with a paper towel the excess liquid. Refrigerate until firm. Cut into rounds. Serve with your favorite breads.

½ cup very finely chopped
  fresh or frozen cranberries
1 cup butter, softened
⅓ cup powdered sugar
Freshly grated rind of one
  orange

Sri Lankan Cranberry Chutney

In 1973, I took a class called "Ceylonese Cooking!" The teachers were a Sri Lankan woman and her American husband. (Sri Lanka was called Ceylon at the time.) They taught us how to make a "basic" chutney recipe which we made with dates, pineapple, and of all things, cranberries! Who would have guessed almost thirty years later I would be revising this for a cranberry cookbook. It is delicious—a little bit sweet, spicy and hot. It is a fabulous twist to the common cranberry sauce!

FOR THE BASIC CHUTNEY MIX:
Blend all ingredients. This mixture can be stored in the refrigerator for up to 4 months.

TO MAKE THE SRI LANKAN CRANBERRY CHUTNEY:
Rinse and drain the cranberries. Discard any bad ones. Place the cranberries, sugar, water and 2 tablespoons of the chutney mix in a 2-quart saucepan. Cook over medium-low heat, stirring often, until the mixture begins to thicken and the majority of the cranberries have popped open. Cool and store in tightly sealed jars in the refrigerator.

BASIC CHUTNEY MIX:
8 whole Japanese red chilies,
  broken into pieces and
  seeds removed
½ ounce fresh ginger, peeled
  and diced
1 large garlic clove, diced
¼ cup white wine vinegar
1 teaspoon salt

SRI LANKAN CRANBERRY MIX:
One 12-ounce bag fresh or
  frozen cranberries
1 cup white sugar
  (or more to your taste)
⅓ cup water
2 tablespoons *Basic Chutney
  Mix* (recipe above)

Sri Lankan Chutney (photo page 68)

In 1816, Henry Hall, a sea captain from Dennis on Cape Cod, became the first grower to commercially cultivate cranberries. He noticed that wild cranberries on his land grew better when the beach sand blew over them. He began transplanting cranberry vines, fencing them in and covering them with sand. Knowledge of his techniques quickly spread, and so did the cranberry industry. Cape Cod became the birthplace of the cranberry industry.

Chapter Two

....

Salads and Salad Dressings

Cranberry Vinegar

MAKES ABOUT 3 CUPS

2 cups fresh or frozen
cranberries, rinsed
3 cups rice vinegar
3 tablespoons sugar

Clear vinegar boiled with cranberries turns bright red and absorbs the fruit's flavor. The blend makes attractive holiday gifts in decorative bottles.

In a 2 to 3 quart pan, on high heat, bring cranberries, vinegar and the sugar to a boil. Simmer, covered, until cranberries pop and are soft, about 5 minutes. Add more sugar to taste, if desired. Let stand until cool. Pour vinegar through a fine strainer into a container with a pouring lip; discard residue. Pour vinegar into sterilized decorative bottles, using a funnel if necks are narrow. Seal with lids. Use, or store at room temperature up to 4 months. If an opaque film develops on surface, spoon it off or, to preserve clarity of vinegar, pour vinegar through a fine strainer into a 2 to 3 quart pan and bring to boiling. Wash bottle, then refill with vinegar. Store as before.

— *Sunset Magazine, December 1992.*

The 1996 United States cranberry harvest yielded 230 billion cranberries—forty-one cranberries for every man, woman and child on earth!

Cranberry Raspberry Vinaigrette

MAKES 6-8 OUNCES • ENOUGH FOR 6 SIDE SALADS

¼ cup raspberry vinegar
⅓ cup walnut oil
⅓ cup whole cranberries
2 tablespoons sugar
Pinch of salt

In a blender combine all the ingredients. Blend until smooth.

Cranberry Vinaigrette

MAKES 6-8 OUNCES • ENOUGH FOR 6 SIDE SALADS

¼ cup frozen cranberry juice
concentrate
⅓ cup vegetable oil
½ teaspoon Dijon-style
prepared mustard
Pinch of salt
¼ cup apple cider, white wine
or rice vinegar

In a blender combine all of the ingredients. Blend until smooth.

Ocean Spray Cranberries photograph

Cranberries flow at the Ocean Spray receiving facility in Carver, MA. During harvest season, a steady convoy of trucks haul millions of pounds to the station, get in line, weigh-in, and unload.

Mixed Baby Greens with Dried Cranberries

SERVES 6

Combine the greens, pecans, cranberries and apple in a large salad bowl. Gently toss with the *Cranberry Vinaigrette*.

8 cups mixed baby greens, washed
¾ cup dry roasted pecans
¾ cup dried cranberries
1 large crispy apple, thinly sliced (Granny Smith, Braeburn, Fuji)
¾ cup Cranberry Vinaigrette or Cranberry-Raspberry Vinaigrette

"Refreshing, cheering, encouraging…" is the description Henry David Thoreau used to describe the cranberry's flavor in an 1852 journal entry. Cranberries are "perhaps the prettiest berry," he observed.

Wilted Spinach Salad with Dried Cranberries, Pecans and Feta Cheese

SERVES 6

*Wilted Spinach Salad
(photo page 76)*

Tossing this salad with hot olive oil causes it to wilt just enough to soften and bring out a bright green color in the spinach.

Quarter and thinly slice the red onion. Place the slices in cold water and allow to soak for 30 minutes. Drain and pat dry. Meanwhile, make the croutons. Brush the bread slices with olive oil. Toast the slices in a 375° oven until nicely browned. Peel the garlic clove and smash it. Rub the browned slices of bread with the garlic after they come out of the oven. Set the croutons aside. Place the soaked onion slices, spinach, pecans, feta, cranberries, mint and vinegar in a large mixing bowl. Toss together with a large pinch of salt. In a saucepan, heat the olive oil to just below smoking. Pour the hot oil over the salad in the bowl, tossing well as you do. Taste and correct the seasoning with salt, pepper and vinegar. Serve with croutons.

— *Drew Spangler, Mill Valley, CA*

SALAD:
1 small red onion
8-9 cups spinach leaves, washed and patted dry
½ cup pecan halves, toasted and very coarsely chopped
4 ounces feta cheese, crumbled
¼ cup dried cranberries
1 tablespoon mint leaves, chopped
2 tablespoons sherry vinegar
Pinch of salt
6 tablespoons olive oil
Black pepper, freshly ground

GARLIC CROUTONS:
Olive oil
1 large garlic clove
12 thin slices baguette or other artisanal bread

Jello molds are back!

These "retro" dishes were popular in the late forties and fifties. Fill them with lots of fresh fruit, vegetables and nuts, and these molds are healthy, colorful, refreshing, and so easy to make! They are great to accompany poultry dishes any time of year.

Raspberry Cranberry Mold
(photo page 78)

One 6-ounce package
  raspberry jello
2 cups boiling water
One 8-ounce can
  whole cranberry sauce
2 cups sour cream

Raspberry Cranberry Mold

SERVE WELL-CHILLED

"It's so easy it should be criminal", is how my friend and author Christine Anderson describes this "Fifties" traditional jello mold. She said it receives rave reviews, especially during the holiday season.

Combine the jello and water. Mix until the jello is dissolved. Cool slightly. Before the jello hardens add the cranberry sauce. When almost set, add the sour cream. Pour into a decorative mold and chill until set.

Zippy Cranberry Mold

SERVES 8-10 · CAN EASILY BE DOUBLED

One 6-ounce package
  cranberry or raspberry jello
2 cups boiling water
One 16-ounce can whole
  cranberry sauce
1 cup canned crushed
  pineapple, drained
¾ cup diced celery
¼ cup diced red pepper
¼ cup diced green pepper
¾ cup chopped pecans or
  walnuts

Dissolve the jello in the boiling water. Add all the other ingredients. Pour into a mold or casserole dish. Chill at least 8 hours or overnight.

— *Bonnie Croopnick, Newton, MA*

Sprinklers at work on A. D. Makepeace's Morse Swamp bog, East Wareham, MA.

Joseph D. Thomas photograph

Sour Cream Cranberry Ring

This recipe comes from a cookbook published by members of Theta Delta Xi, a non-academic sorority established fifty years ago. They are dedicated to raising funds for national associations for special needs children. This recipe was given to me by Helen Spivock, one of the founding members and Lee Labe Pollak, daughter of founding member Arnette Labe Stark.

Dissolve the jello in the water. Add lemon juice and cranberry sauce. Stir to mix well. Pour into a greased jello mold. Refrigerate. When slightly thickened, mix in the sour cream. Cool until set.

One 6-ounce package cherry
flavored jello
1 cup hot water
1 tablespoon fresh lemon juice
2 16-ounce cans jellied
cranberry sauce
1 pint sour cream

Crunchy Cranberry Salad Mold

SERVES 8-10 • CAN EASILY BE DOUBLED

Dissolve the jello in the water. Add the sugar, lemon juice and pineapple juice. Stir well. Add the remaining ingredients. Pour into a mold or casserole dish. Refrigerate at least 8 hours or overnight.

— *Wendy Delgado, Wrangler, Alisal Ranch, Solvang, CA*

*Recipes for cooking with cranberries were very limited in the
1940s and 1950s. Jello molds using cranberry sauce were very popular,
particularly during the holiday season.*

One 6-ounce package
cranberry or cherry jello
1 cup boiling water
¼ cup sugar
1 tablespoon fresh lemon juice
1 cup pineapple juice
1 cup chopped fresh or frozen
cranberries
1 cup crushed pineapple,
drained
1 cup chopped celery
1 orange, seeds removed and
coarsely chopped
½ cup walnuts, finely chopped

Ocean Spray Cranberries photograph

A Model-A truck is used for ice sanding on one of Alex Johnson's bogs in South Carver, MA, 1926. Before helicopters, growers did winter sanding by spreading an even layer of sand on the ice, then they waited for the ice to melt. This old sanding truck had a self-propelled tip cart; its drive mechanism can be seen on the rear left wheel.

Pan Pacific Chicken Salad with Cranberries, Almonds & Pineapple

MAKES ⅔ CUP DRESSING · SERVES 6

Combine all of the ingredients for the salad in a large serving bowl. Whisk together all the ingredients for the dressing. Toss the dressing gently into the salad. Serve chilled.

CHICKEN SALAD:

6 boneless chicken breasts, grilled, poached or roasted and diced (or 6 cups diced cooked chicken)

1 fresh pineapple (about 4 cups) or two 16-ounce cans pineapple chunks, drained

¾ cup slivered almonds, lightly roasted

¾ cup dried cranberries

3 green onions (only the green part) finely diced

⅛ cup cilantro, finely chopped

DRESSING:

¼ cup rice vinegar

1 tablespoon plus 1 teaspoon dark soy sauce

1 tablespoon sesame oil

¼ cup vegetable oil

1 teaspoon sugar

Old screenhouse used for storage on a cranberry bog in Wareham, MA.

John K. Robson photograph

Albacore Tuna with Dill and Dried Cranberries

MAKES 4 SERVINGS

The yogurt helps to make this recipe lower in fat as well as delicious.

Drain the tuna well and put in a bowl with the mayonnaise, yogurt, lemon juice, dill weed, salt, garlic powder and lemon pepper. Mix until well blended. Add the apple, celery and cranberries. Serve as a sandwich on bread, toast, a bagel or English muffin, or serve as a salad on a bed of lettuce or spinach with your favorite salad dressing.

Two 6-ounce cans white albacore tuna in water

2 tablespoons mayonnaise

2 tablespoons low-fat plain yogurt

1 teaspoon lemon juice

1 teaspoon dill weed

¼ teaspoon salt

½ teaspoon garlic powder

½ teaspoon lemon pepper

½ cup finely chopped apple

¼ cup finely chopped celery

⅓ cup dried cranberries

Cranberry Slaw

MAKES 8 SERVINGS

This fresh salad is beautifully colorful, healthy, easy to prepare and delicious!

Combine the cabbage, carrots, onion and cranberries in a large salad or mixing bowl. Whisk together all the other ingredients in a small bowl. Pour over the cabbage mixture and toss until well mixed. Serve immediately, or keep covered in the refrigerator overnight.

4 cups shredded red cabbage (about ½ medium head)
2 cups shredded carrots (about 3 medium)
½ red onion, thinly sliced
¾ cup dried cranberries
¼ cup apple cider vinegar
⅔ cup olive oil
1 tablespoon prepared Dijon-style mustard
1 tablespoon caraway seeds
1 teaspoon sugar
½ teaspoon salt
⅛ teaspoon ground black pepper

Old screenhouse no longer in use at the Federal Furnace Cranberry Co.

John K. Robson photograph

Cranberry Waldorf Salad

SERVES 6-8

This favorite from the fifties takes a new turn with the addition of cranberries for taste and color and a light, low-fat, citrus and honey dressing.

Combine all the ingredients for the salad in a large serving bowl. Whisk together the ingredients for the dressing. Toss the dressing gently into the salad. Serve chilled over a bed of lettuce.

SALAD:
4 cups crisp apples, chopped
1 cup celery, chopped
1 cup green or red seedless grapes, halved
¾ cup dried cranberries
¾ cup chopped walnuts

DRESSING:
¼ cup low-fat plain yogurt
2 tablespoons orange juice
1 tablespoon lemon juice
1 tablespoon honey
¼ teasponn salt

Chapter Three

....

Vegetables, Grains and Stuffings

Couscous with Dried Cranberries, Pine Nuts and Fresh Mint

SERVES 6

One 12-ounce package couscous

One 14-ounce can chicken or vegetable broth

Pinch of salt

3 tablespoons walnut, almond or olive oil

1 teaspoon fresh lemon juice

¾ cup dried cranberries

⅓ cup pine nuts

⅓ cup fresh mint leaves

Serve as a delicious side dish with lamb, poultry, or fish.

Cook the couscous according to the package directions, using broth instead of water. Add a pinch of salt to the broth.

While it is cooking, roast the pine nuts in a very low (250°) oven for 10 minutes or until lightly browned. Wash and finely chop the mint leaves. When the couscous has finished cooking, drain any excess liquid. If more liquid is needed to cook the couscous, add water, a little at a time. Pour the couscous into a serving bowl. Add the oil and the lemon juice. Stir well to coat all the grains. Add the cranberries, pine nuts and mint leaves. Stir to combine all the ingredients. Serve immediately.

*Couscous with Dried Cranberries
(photo page 76)*

Wild Rice with Dried Cranberries and Roasted Pecans

SERVES 6-8

4 cups cooked wild rice

¼ cup walnut or olive oil

2 tablespoons orange juice

2 tablespoons raspberry vinegar

4 scallions, diced

½ teaspoon salt

Grated zest of one orange

¾ cup dried cranberries

¾ cup oven roasted pecan pieces

This is a delicious side dish for pork, poultry or fish.

In a serving bowl add all the ingredients to the wild rice, stirring after each addition. Let stand for a few hours or overnight. Keep refrigerated if stored overnight. Serve at room temperature.

Thanksgiving greeting card, circa 1925

GOOD WISHES FOR THANKSGIVING DAY

Nancy Cappelloni

Tangerine Yams with Cranberries

MAKES 10 SERVINGS

The tangerine brings a new twist to this elegant dish.

Preheat oven to 350°.
Cut the yams into quarters and boil in a large pot of salted water for 15 minutes or until soft. Drain well and peel skins. Cut yams into large chunks. In a large mixing bowl or food processor with the metal knife in place, combine the yams and the 3 peeled and seeded tangerines. Process until smooth. Add the butter, brown sugar, cinnamon, nutmeg and rum. Continue to process until the yams are pureed. Gently mix in the cranberries. Pour the mixture into a buttered 2½-quart casserole or baking dish. Bake covered for 40 minutes at 350°. Garnish with tangerine slices. Serve immediately.

3 pounds yams
3 tangerines, peeled and
  seeded
1 cup fresh or frozen whole
  cranberries
4 tablespoons butter, melted
⅔ cup brown sugar
¼ teaspoon cinnamon
¼ teaspoon nutmeg
2 tablespoons rum (optional)
1 tangerine, sliced for garnish

No American Thanksgiving dinner would

seem complete without cranberries, or for that matter, without

yams or sweet potatoes. Cranberries and pumpkins are among the

many foods believed to have been served at the first feast of 1621,

but yams are presumably a more recent addition.

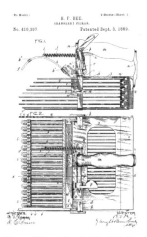

Patent illustration for the B. F. Bee Cranberry Picker or "snap scoop," 1890.
— Courtesy of Nancy Davison.

Thanksgiving celebration at historic Plimoth Plantation in Plymouth, MA, 1962.

Spinner Collection

Surprise Noodle Kugel

MAKES 10-12 SERVINGS

KUGEL:

One 12-ounce bag medium
   egg noodles
One 8-ounce package cream
   cheese, softened
6 tablespoons butter, room
   temperature
2 tablespoons sugar
4 eggs well-beaten
1 cup milk, heated but not
   boiled
1 cup apricot nectar
⅔ cup dried cranberries

TOPPING:

2 cups crushed corn flakes
1 teaspoon cinnamon
3 tablespoons butter, room
   temperature
2 tablespoons sugar

The surprise in this creamy noodle kugel is the dried cranberries that replace the traditional raisins used in most kugel, or noodle pudding recipes. The cranberries add color and a slight tartness to my mother's traditional Jewish holiday dish.

Preheat oven to 375°.

Cook the noodles in boiling salted water. Drain. In a large mixing bowl cream together the cream cheese, butter and sugar. Add the eggs, the milk and apricot nectar. Stir in the cranberries. Add the noodles. The mixture will be slightly liquidy. Pour into a buttered two-quart casserole or baking dish. Mix together the ingredients for the topping. Sprinkle the topping evenly over the kugel. Bake in a 375° oven for 25 minutes. Cover with foil and cook for another 15-20 minutes.

Only twelve to fifteen percent of all cranberries are sold fresh.

The remaining eighty-two to eighty-five percent of cranberries are processed

into juice, sauce and processed foods.

Harvest Butternut Squash Medley

MAKES 6 SERVINGS

3-4 pounds butternut squash
1 small red onion, diced
   (about 1 cup diced)
2 tablespoons olive oil
½ cup dried cranberries
Fresh seeds from 1
   pomegranate
¼ cup roasted pumpkin seeds
1 tablespoon sherry wine
   vinegar
1 tablespoon molasses
¼ teaspoon salt
Dash of pepper

Preheat oven to 375°.

With a strong knife, quarter the squash and remove the seeds. Microwave the squash, covered, for 6 minutes in a microwave safe dish filled with 2 tablespoons water. Cool for 5 minutes. Peel the skin and discard. Cube the squash. Dice the red onion. Place the squash and onion in a baking or roasting dish. Add the oil. Bake at 375° for 30 minutes. Remove the pan from the oven and cool. Add the dried cranberries, pomegranate seeds and pumpkin seeds. Toss. Add the vinegar, molasses, salt and pepper. Gently toss. Transfer to a serving dish and serve at room temperature or chilled.

Depending on the size of the squash, you may want to vary the amounts of the oil, vinegar, molasses, cranberries and pumpkin seeds to taste.

Acorn Squash with Cranberry Filling

MAKES 8 SERVINGS

Serve as a side dish with poultry, game or pork.

Cut the squash in half lengthwise. Remove the seeds. Place the squash, cut sides down, on a buttered baking sheet. Bake for 30 minutes in a 375° oven. Combine the cranberries, pecans, brown sugar, butter, orange marmalade and cinnamon. Turn the squash cut sides up on the baking sheet. Fill each squash with the cranberry mixture. Cover with aluminum foil. Bake for 45 minutes at 350° or until squash is tender.

The natural waxy coating on the cranberry

helps to keep them fresh over long periods of time.

4 acorn squash
1 cup coarsely chopped
    cranberries
¾ cup chopped pecans
½ cup brown sugar
½ cup butter, melted
½ cup orange marmalade
½ teaspoon ground cinnamon

Acorn Squash with Filling
(photo page 72)

"Pudding in the Belly" Cranberry Stuffing

MAKES ENOUGH FOR ONE 15-POUND TURKEY
PLUS 1 CASSEROLE DISH

Even into the nineteenth century most English cookbooks concentrated on the preparation of meat, fish, fowl and game. Cranberries are known to have been added to "puddings" which were then stuffed in the "belly" or cavity of many kinds of fowl. This contemporary version of "Pudding in the Belly" provides an interesting twist to your traditional Thanksgiving stuffing, whether cooked in or out of the "belly".

IF USING CORNBREAD:

Cut the cornbread into ½" cubes. Don't worry if it becomes crumbly and falls apart. Use all of it anyway. Add all the other ingredients (except for the orange juice) to the cornbread. Toss until well-mixed. Add the orange juice to moisten the mixture so that it barely holds together.

Use as you would for stuffing a turkey or for baking on the side. If baking as a side dish, put the stuffing in a casserole or loaf pan and cover. Baste with cooking juices from your turkey or other fowl. Cook for one hour at 350°. The stuffing can be made ahead and kept in the refrigerator for 2 days or in the freezer. If frozen, thaw before using. Add the orange juice just before you use the stuffing.

1 prepared loaf or pan of
    corn bread, or one 12-
    ounce package prepared
    cornbread stuffing mix
½ teaspoon thyme
½ teaspoon sage
¼ teaspoon ground black
    pepper
¼ teaspoon paprika
1 large or 2 small crisp apples,
    peeled, cored and coarsely
    chopped (about 1½ cups)
1 small white or yellow onion,
    diced (about ¾ cup)
3 stalks of celery, diced
½ cup dried cranberries,
    chopped
½ cup whole hazelnuts, halved
¾ cup orange juice

Photo Gallery
of
Dishes and Harvests

In the spring, the cranberry flower covers the bog with a soft pastel blanket of white and pink. During winter, the grower sanded and weeded, dug-out trenches, applied herbicides and managed his irrigation network. With the right mixture of sun and rain, and with help from bees brought in to pollinate the flower, he'll have a good crop.

Joseph D. Thomas photograph

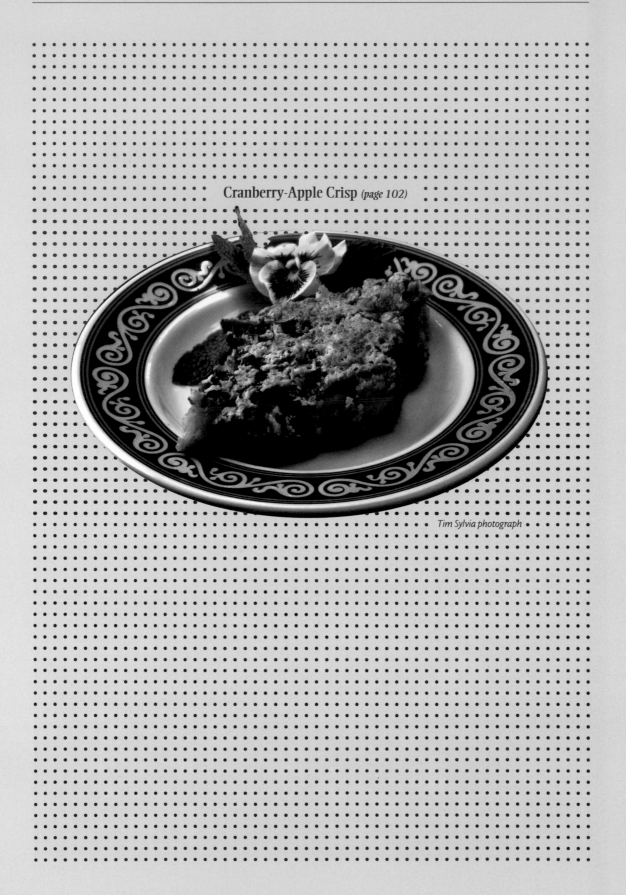

Cranberry-Apple Crisp *(page 102)*

Tim Sylvia photograph

Cranberry Applesauce Muffins *(page 125)* and Cranberry Orange Scones *(page 129)*

Tim Sylvia photograph

Sri Lankan Cranberry Chutney *(page 49)*

Tim Sylvia photograph

Fresh Cranberry Orange Relish *(page 46)*

Tim Sylvia photograph

Nantucket Roast Loin of Pork with Cranberry Cornbread Stuffing *(page 83)*

Tim Sylvia photograph

John K. Robson photograph   *Joseph D. Thomas photograph*

Bountiful Harvest

Cranberries knocked free from the vines by the water-reel harvester (top left), float on the flooded bog. They will be raked into the mouth of a suction device that feeds them into the hopper of an 18-wheeler, and trucked to the processing plant. The dry-picked berries at right will be screened from the chaff, sorted and packaged fresh. Below, friends have brought home fresh berries that they used to make sauces, salad, stuffing and bread for a Saturday night feast.

Tim Sylvia photograph

Assorted cranberry box labels, 1930–1960.

Acorn Squash with Cranberry Filling *(page 63)*

Tim Sylvia photograph

Muscovy Duck Breasts in Sherry, Port and Cranberries *(page 90)*

Tim Sylvia photograph

John K. Robson photograph

Little Bog, Big Bog

In Southeastern Massachusetts, many cranberry bogs are small, owner-operated farms nestled between woodlands and cedar swamps. In the scene above, Steve Ashley, owner of My Achin' Back Bog in East Freetown, and his dog, Boy, look for muskrat holes and ditches that might disable the water-reel harvester operated by Steve Bottomley. Below, water-reels are hard at work at Milestone Bog on Nantucket. This 280-acre bog, built in 1900, is the largest contiguous bog in the world.

Joseph D. Thomas photograph

Cranberry Raspberry Slump *(page 97)*

Tim Sylvia photograph

An old screenhouse at the Federal Furnace Cranberry Company in Carver, MA, is a reminder of the days when most berries were dry harvested and screenhouses were bustling with production. Today, screenhouses are largely a remnant of the past.

The young birch woodland that surrounds bogs of the Federal Furnace Company represent an essential component of the cranberry-growing environment. Adjacent forests and wetlands nourish the watershed and buffer the fragile growing areas from both natural and man-made encroachment.

John K. Robson photograph

John K. Robson photograph

Cranberry Nut Tart *(page 102)*

Tim Sylvia photograph

Couscous with Dried Cranberries, Pine Nuts and Fresh Mint *(page 60)*

Tim Sylvia photograph

Wilted Spinach Salad with Dried Cranberries, Pecans and Feta Cheese *(page 53)*

Tim Sylvia photograph

The Dry Harvest

All cranberries sold fresh at the market are dry harvested. In these scenes at the Stuart Bog in Rochester, Massachusetts, the cranberry's journey from the bog to your dinner table begins. Hard at work in the crisp October sun (left), workers for Decas Brothers Cranberries use mechanical harvesters that scoop the berries from the thick vines and convey them into burlap bags attached beneath the machine's handles. When the bag is filled, it is detached and left on the bog. After completing his rows (center), the worker pours the berries into a large crate set nearby (right). Toward the end of the day, the crates are lifted by helicopter from the bog onto the shore (below), where they will be fork-lifted onto large trucks, sorted and cleaned at the screenhouse, packaged and shipped to market. — *Photographs by Joseph D. Thomas*

Raspberry Cranberry Mold *(page 54)*

Photographs by Tim Sylvia

Drinks *(pages 131–135)*

California Cranberry-Berry Smoothie *(page 132)*

Tim Sylvia photograph

Chapter Four

....

Poultry, Pork, Game and Meat

Buffalo Steaks with Cranberry, Chipotle Chili and Sage Sauce

SERVES 4

4 buffalo steaks
1 tablespoon olive oil

SAUCE:
1 tablespoon olive oil
1 large shallot, minced
1 large clove garlic, minced
1 cup cranberries, fresh or
    frozen
1 tablespoon honey
1 tablespoon sugar
½ cup dry red wine
½ cup beef stock
½ chipotle chili (a dried, smoked
    jalapeño chili)*
Pinch of salt
1 tablespoon fresh sage, finely
    chopped or 1½ teaspoons
    dried sage
Fresh sage leaves for garnish

If chipotle chilies are not available use whole dried red chilies with the seeds removed.

FOR PAN FRYING:

Place a large sauté pan over high heat. When the pan is hot, brush with 1 tablespoon of the oil. Pan fry the steaks until they are cooked to a desired doneness. Remove them from the pan and keep them warm while you make the sauce.

FOR GRILLING:

Grill the steaks to a desired doneness. Keep steaks warm while you make the sauce.

FOR THE SAUCE:

Reheat the sauté pan and add 1 tablespoon olive oil. Add the shallots and garlic and cook over medium heat until translucent, taking care not to burn the garlic. Add the cranberries, honey, sugar, wine and beef stock. Scrape the pan to loosen any bits from the bottom of the pan. Bring the sauce to a boil, reduce to a simmer and cook, stirring often, until the majority of the cranberries pop open and the sauce begins to thicken, about 10 minutes.

Place the sauce in a blender. Crush some of the chili and add a little of it to the sauce and blend. Taste. Add more chili as desired. Blend well and taste after each addition until the desired heat is reached. Add the pinch of salt. Remove the sauce from the blender. Add the chopped sage. Pour any juices that may have accumulated under the cooked steaks into the sauce.

TO SERVE:

Serve ¼ cup of the sauce on top of or alongside each steak. Garnish with additional sage leaves.

— Adapted from a recipe by Drew Spangler, Mill Valley, CA

Eastman Johnson's painting, circa 1872, shows a lone cranberry harvester near the dunes on Nantucket.

Cranberries have been grown on Nantucket since 1857 and were an important part of the Island's economy until just prior to World War II. Before 1959, all 234 acres of bog were under cultivation on the Milestone Road, making this bog the largest contiguous natural cranberry bog in the world.

UMass Cranberry Experiment Station

Nantucket Roast Loin of Pork
with Cranberry Cornbread Stuffing

SERVES 15

Preheat oven to 375°.

Cut a slit along the center of each of the tenderloins to create a pocket. In a large mixing bowl, break the cornbread into small pieces. Sauté the onions and celery in the butter until soft. Add the cranberries and heat until the cranberries just begin to pop. Stir the cranberry mixture into the cornbread and mix lightly. Cool one half hour. Add the eggs, the sage, salt and pepper. Combine well. Fill each pocket with the stuffing. Place the tenderloins in a roasting pan. Pour half the *Cranberry Orange Maple Glaze* over them. Cover with foil and bake for one hour. Remove the foil, pour the remaining glaze on the tenderloins and continue to bake uncovered for another half hour, or until the meat is done. Cut into slices and serve immediately.

— Adapted from a recipe by Nantucket Island Chamber of Commerce

John Josselyn, an Englishman visiting New England in 1638

and again in 1663, wrote in detail of the animals

and plants which he found in "the new land." He wrote, "…The

Indians and English use them (cranberries) much, boyling them with

Sugar for Sauce to eat with their Meate, and it is a

delicate Sauce, especially for Roast Mutton."

5 one-pound pork tenderloins
4 cups cornbread, broken into
    small pieces
1 cup finely chopped yellow
    onion
1 cup finely chopped celery
3 eggs, well beaten
¼ cup butter
1 pound cranberries
2 tablespoons dried sage
1 teaspoon salt
½ teaspoon ground black
    pepper
*Cranberry Orange Maple
    Glaze* (see recipe below)

Nantucket Roast Loin of Pork
(photo page 69)

Cranberry Orange Maple Glaze

MAKES 1¼ CUPS GLAZE

This versatile glaze can be used for glazing and basting a turkey, ham, pork loin, or other kinds of poultry or game. It is easy to prepare and uses ingredients available year round.

Combine ingredients in a small saucepan and cook over medium heat. Bring to a simmer. Stir until a thick glaze forms, about 3-5 minutes.

Store in the refrigerator. It will keep up to two weeks.

½ cup jellied cranberry sauce,
    mashed
¼ cup cranberry juice
¼ cup orange juice
¼ cup pure maple syrup
¼ teaspoon ground ginger
½ teaspoon dry mustard

Oven Roasted Cornish Game Hens with Cranberry Orange Maple Glaze

SERVES 6

3 Cornish game hens, halved lengthwise

1 cup *Cranberry Orange Maple Glaze* (page 83)

Preheat oven to 400°.

Place the hens on a baking sheet or roasting pan, cut side down. Brush each hen generously with the glaze and put into the oven. Bake, uncovered, for 15 minutes. Reduce the heat to 350°. Brush the hens with the glaze again and cook for 45-55 minutes more, basting every 15 minutes. The hens will be done when the skin has browned and the juices run clear from the thigh when pierced with a fork.

Oven Braised Ribs

SERVES 4-6

2½ - 3 pounds pork backribs or beef backribs

4 cups onions, sliced

4 cloves garlic, finely diced

1 tablespoon vegetable oil

⅔ cup cider vinegar

½ cup water

3 tablespoons Worcestershire sauce

2 tablespoons brown sugar

¼ teaspoon chili powder

¼ teaspoon ground black pepper

1 teaspoon ground mustard powder

2 cups (16-ounce can) jellied cranberry sauce

This recipe has been adapted from Dorothy "Dot" Angley's cranberry recipe book called The Full Scoop. *With her husband, Mrs. Angley operates Flax Pond Cranberry Farm in Carver, Massachusetts. For many years, Dot was in charge of the cranberry recipe contest at the Massachusetts Cranberry Harvest Festival.*

Bake the ribs in a shallow pan at 450° for 30 minutes. Drain off the fat. While the ribs are cooking, heat the oil in a saucepan and sauté the onions and garlic until almost translucent. Add the remaining ingredients and simmer for 10 minutes. Take the ribs out of the oven and cover with the cranberry mixture. Reduce oven to 350°. Cook for 20 minutes. Cover and cook for 40 more minutes, turning the ribs once or twice during baking. Serve ribs with the sauce and lots of napkins.

Dry harvesting on Decas Brothers Cranberries' Stuart Bog.

Joseph D. Thomas photograph

Cornish Game Hens
with Cranberry Stuffing

SERVES 6

These beautifully glazed birds look like miniature Thanksgiving turkeys.

No wonder Joy of Cooking (Rombauer and Becker, 1931), one of our earliest American cookbooks, explains that Rock Cornish Game Hens are a result of cross-breeding between Cornish gamecocks and Plymouth Rock hens! Additionally, their gamy flavor is due partly to their ancestry and partly to a diet that usually includes acorns and cranberries!

Prepare the *Pudding in the Belly Cranberry Stuffing.* Rinse and clean the cavity of each game hen. Prepare the *Spiced Cranberry Glaze.* Preheat oven to 400°. Fill each hen with about ¾ cup of the stuffing. Close the opening using a small metal skewer. (Be sure to stuff the hens just before roasting.) Place the hens in a large roasting pan, breast sides up. Brush some of the glaze on each hen. Put the hens in the oven. Bake for 20 minutes. Take the hens out and brush with more glaze. Reduce oven to 350°. Baste frequently with the pan juices (every 15-20 minutes). Continue to cook for another hour and one half, or until the juices run clear when the meat of the thigh is pierced. Total cooking time will be between 1½-2 hours, depending on the size of the hens. Remove metal skewers and serve warm, drizzle with *Glaze.*

If you prefer to cook the stuffing separately, place it in a loaf pan and bake for one hour in the oven with the hens. The hens will cook in less time. Check for doneness after an hour to an hour-and-a-quarter.

6 Cornish game hens
"Pudding in the Belly"
 Cranberry Stuffing (page 63)
Spiced Cranberry Glaze (page 48)

Most of the world's cranberries are cultivated on approximately 30,000 acres in just five states—Massachusetts, Wisconsin, New Jersey, Oregon and Washington. Another 3,000 acres are cultivated in British Columbia. Within the last several years cranberry growing and processing can be found in South America, as well as in eastern Europe and Russia.

Water-harvesting in South Carver, MA. Corralled berries are being pulled toward one end of the bog where they will be taken out.

Joseph D. Thomas photograph

Pork Chops with Simmered Cranberries

SERVES 4

4 center cut pork loin chops
1 cup diced celery
¼ teaspoon salt
3 tablespoons vegetable oil
½ cup all-purpose flour
Freshly grated rind of one
  orange
½ cup sugar
2 cups fresh or frozen
  cranberries, coarsely
  chopped
2 tablespoons medium or dry
  Sherry (optional)
1 orange, thinly sliced

In a large skillet, frying pan or sauté pan, sauté the celery in 1 tablespoon oil for 5 minutes or until soft. Mix in the salt. Remove the celery from the pan. Lightly coat each pork chop in the flour. Sauté the pork chops in the remaining oil on medium heat 4-5 minutes per side to lightly brown. Reduce the heat to low. Return the celery to the pan along with the pork chops. Mix the cranberries with the sugar. Add them to the pan. Sprinkle on the orange rind. Cover and simmer for 10 minutes. Turn the pork chops over, stir the cranberries and simmer for another 10 minutes. Add the Sherry. Return to a simmer.

Serve each pork chop with the cranberry and celery mixture, topped with a slice of orange.

Sautéed Chicken with Cranberries and Apple Cider Reduction

MAKES 4 SERVINGS

Four 6-ounce boneless
  chicken breasts
¼ cup flour
¼ cup oil
1 tablespoon shallots, peeled
  and chopped
½ cup fresh or frozen
  cranberries, chopped
½ cup chicken stock
¼ cup white wine
1 tablespoon sugar
¼ cup apple cider
2 tablespoons unsalted butter

Roasted potatoes or buttered rice with freshly steamed green beans will make a full plate.

Dust the chicken with flour, one at a time, shaking off any excess. Heat the oil in a large sauté pan over medium-high heat, then sauté the chicken until golden brown on both sides and thoroughly cooked, 3-5 minutes each side. Transfer the chicken to a serving platter and hold warm. Pour off any remaining oil. Put the pan back on the heat and toss in the shallots and cranberries. Cook for 2 minutes. Add stock and wine, bring to a low boil and reduce volume by half. Stir in sugar and cider and reduce by half. Pour over chicken breasts.

The butter can be deleted for a lower fat recipe.

— New Bedford gourmet chef, Stephen Worden
from Out of the Earth *by Kerry Downey Romaniello*

The first published cookbook of American foods, American Cookery, *published in 1796, suggested serving roast stuffed turkey or fowl with cranberry sauce.*

Chicken with Honey and Dried Fruit

SERVES 6-8

In Israeli tradition, honey symbolizes the sweetness of the New Year or any other joyous occasion. Chicken is commonly cooked with oranges and honey in Israel since oranges are one of its largest crops. Many variations of "Oaf Tapuzim," chicken with oranges, have been created throughout the Middle East. Dried fruit and honey are commonly added to the chicken to create a sweet, stewed dish.

Combine marinade ingredients. In a large baking pan or casserole pour the marinade over the chicken pieces, coating all sides. In a separate bowl combine the orange juice, lemon juice and brown sugar. Add the dried apples, dried apricots and dried cranberries. Put both bowls in refrigerator, covered, for several hours or overnight.

WHEN READY TO COOK:

In a large pot heat the oil. Add the chicken. Brown on all sides about 10 minutes. Add the marinade. Bring to a boil. Cover and simmer for 10 minutes. Turn the pieces of chicken over. Simmer for 10 more minutes. Pour the dried fruit and their juices over the cooking chicken. Cover and simmer 10 more minutes. Serve the chicken immediately with the fruit and cooking juices over rice, couscous, polenta or other grain.

4-5 pounds chicken breasts and thighs, cut into pieces and skinned (about 10 pieces)

MARINADE INGREDIENTS:
1 cup white wine
2 tablespoons honey
2 tablespoons ginger root, diced
1 teaspoon paprika
1 teaspoon ground cinnamon
¼ teaspoon ground black pepper

TO COOK CHICKEN:
1 cup orange juice
1 tablespoon fresh lemon juice
2 tablespoons brown sugar
1 cup dried apples
1 cup dried apricots
1 cup dried cranberries
2 tablespoons olive oil

Middleborough Public Library

Sorting berries at Ellis D. Atwood's South Carver screenhouse, 1938. After the berries are screened from chaff and soft, damaged berries, they are transported by conveyor to the sorting area. Sorting berries simply means removing the unwanted ones. Berries that are not colored properly or are imperfect in some way, are taken out one by one by the screeners. It is a tedious job that demands complete concentration. The women sit in one position for a long period, focusing on thousands of tiny moving objects less than three feet away. A conscientious employer would have excellent lighting and comfortable seating, and allow screeners frequent breaks to relieve eye and back strain.

Grilled Chicken with Caramelized Pecans and Cranberry Raspberry Sauce

SERVES 6 · MAKES ABOUT 2½ CUPS

6 boneless, skinless chicken breasts
¼ cup raspberry vinegar
2 tablespoons olive or vegetable oil

CARAMELIZED PECANS:
1 cup pecan pieces
1 tablespoon butter
2 teaspoons water
¼ cup sugar

CRANBERRY RASPBERRY SAUCE:
3 cups cranberries (12-ounce bag)
1 cup water
1½ cups sugar
One 12-ounce bag frozen raspberries

Marinate the chicken in the vinegar and oil for at least 2 hours or overnight. Prepare the *Cranberry Raspberry Sauce* and the *Caramelized Pecans*. Grill the chicken breasts on a medium-high grill until done. To serve: On each plate place one grilled chicken breast covered with a few spoonfuls of the *Cranberry Raspberry Sauce*. Sprinkle with some *Caramelized Pecans* on top.

CARAMELIZED PECANS:
Melt the butter in a large skillet or frying pan on low heat. Add the pecans and stir, about 2-3 minutes. Add the water and sugar, stirring until the sugar caramelizes and the pecans are evenly coated, about 5 minutes. Cool.

CRANBERRY RASPBERRY SAUCE:
Place the cranberries and water in a medium saucepan or pot. Stir in the sugar and cook on medium heat for 5-10 minutes or until the cranberries have almost all popped open. Add the raspberries and continue to cook about 5 more minutes or until the sauce is well blended.

Researchers from Harvard and Rutgers Universities have correlated the benefits of cranberries in fighting urinary tract infections. Scientists have uncovered hints that the infection fighting powers in cranberries contain a compound that prevents bacteria from attaching to the lining of the urinary bladder.

A polybag packaging machine at Ocean Spray's Middleboro plant, circa 1965.

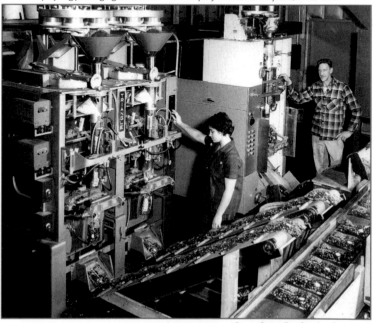

Ocean Spray Cranberries photograph

Squab in Cranberry Marsala Sauce

SERVES 8

Season the squab with salt and pepper. Rub with 1 tablespoon olive oil.

COOKING METHOD I — Heat the grill to medium high. Grill the squabs, turning frequently, every 3-4 minutes. Squabs take about 12 minutes.

COOKING METHOD II — Heat the grill to medium high. Place the squabs skin side down and grill for 4 minutes. Turn the squabs over and cook for 3 more minutes. Take the squabs off the grill, place them in a baking dish, and bake them in a preheated 375° oven for 20 minutes.

COOKING METHOD III — Heat 1 tablespoon olive oil in a large sauté or frying pan. Sauté the squabs on all sides, turning frequently, cooking on medium heat for about 15 minutes, browning the skin nicely. Transfer the squabs to a baking dish and bake in a preheated 375° oven about 15-20 minutes.

CRANBERRY MARSALA SAUCE:

If you have pan fried the squab first, save the juices in the pan after you put the squab in the oven. Deglaze the pan by adding ¼ cup Marsala, and using a wooden spoon or spatula, scraping the bottom of the pan. Add the chicken broth, the cranberries and the sugar. Bring to a boil and then simmer about 15 minutes. Add the remaining ¼ cup Marsala. The sauce will be liquidy. Continue to simmer a few more minutes. Turn the heat off. The sauce will thicken as it cools. If it gets too thick, add more chicken broth and/or Marsala.

If you have only barbecued the squab, bring the chicken broth, cranberries and sugar to a boil in a 2-quart sauce pan or sauté pan. Simmer for 15 minutes. As the sauce begins to thicken, add the Marsala. Simmer a few more minutes.

If you have barbecued **and** roasted the squab, start the sauce when the squab has finished cooking in the oven. In a 2-quart sauce pan or sauté pan, pour in the remaining cooking juices from the squab in the baking dish. To the juices add ¼ cup Marsala and simmer. Add the chicken broth, cranberries and sugar. Simmer for 15 minutes Add the remaining ¼ cup Marsala. Continue to simmer a few more minutes. The sauce will thicken as it cools.

SERVING SUGGESTIONS:

Place a halved squab on a bed of soft polenta. Arrange about ¼ cup of *Cranberry Marsala Sauce* alongside the squab. Place a sprig of fresh thyme on top of the squab.

4 whole squabs, cleaned and split
Salt and pepper
2 tablespoons olive oil
½ cup Marsala wine
½ cup chicken broth
2 cups fresh or frozen whole cranberries
¾ cup sugar
Fresh thyme sprig

The Wampanoag were instrumental in teaching the Pilgrims in America not only how to plant corn and beans and where to pick native berries, but they taught them how to fish and how to cook shellfish. The Wampanoag taught the new settlers the original version of what later became known as the "New England Clambake."

Muscovy Duck Breasts… (photo page 72)

2 pounds boneless Muscovy duck breasts (3-4 breasts; if breasts are large, halve, and trim any excess fat and skin)

3 tablespoons medium dry Sherry

3 tablespoons dark Soy sauce

For the Sauce:

1 cup chicken broth

½ cup plus 2 tablespoons sugar

2 cups whole fresh or frozen cranberries

⅓ cup Port wine

Muscovy Duck Breasts in Sherry, Port and Cranberries

Makes 4-6 servings

Score the duck breasts by making several diagonal cuts in the skin, being careful not to go through the meat. Place the duck in a glass baking dish. Mix the Sherry and Soy and pour over the duck, turning the breasts to coat all sides. Cover and refrigerate at least 2 hours or overnight.

In a medium saucepan combine the chicken broth, sugar and cranberries. Cook over medium low heat about 10 minutes or until the berries have popped and the sauce has begun to thicken. Add the Port and simmer for 5 more minutes. Keep warm.

Remove the duck from the marinade. Heat a large skillet, frying pan or Dutch oven. Cook the breasts on medium heat, skin side down, until the skin begins to get crispy, about 10 minutes. Turn the breasts over and continue to cook, browning the other sides, for 5-10 minutes or to desired doneness and until the skin is crispy. Transfer the duck to a plate covered with paper towels, and keep warm. To serve, place a duck breast on each plate and spoon some of the *Cranberry-Port* sauce over each piece. Serve with roasted potatoes, wild rice or other grain.

An old village of bog houses In South Carver, MA is left to the ages. Throughout the first half of the 20th century, these small shacks housed migrant workers harvesting the bogs from September to November. Although most shacks were designed to house 1–4 people, accounts from 1911 show that as many 12-15 men were packed into a single dwelling (National Child Labor Commission).

John K. Robson photograph

Quail in Cranberry Madeira Sauce

SERVES 2-4

An elegant, colorful meal served with glazed carrots and rice or garlic mashed potatoes.

Preheat oven to 425°.

In a large sauté pan heat the oil. When the oil is hot, brown the quail, turning each one frequently to brown all sides, about 7 minutes. Remove the quail from the pan and place in a baking dish, breast side up, and bake for 10 minutes. Reduce the heat to 375° and cook for 10 more minutes. While the quail are in the oven prepare the sauce. Deglaze the sauté pan by pouring the chicken broth into the pan, scraping the bottom of the pan while cooking on medium high heat. Stir in the cranberries and the sugar. Bring to a boil and simmer for 10-15 minutes until all the berries have popped and the sauce has thickened. Add the Madeira and the thyme, bring back to a simmer and turn off the heat. When the quail are out of the oven, pour any juices that may have accumulated under them into the cranberry sauce, stirring to combine. To serve: Place one or two quails on each plate and spoon some of the *Cranberry Madeira* sauce alongside each quail. Garnish with a sprig of fresh thyme.

1 tablespoon olive oil

4 quail, washed and patted
   dry, legs trussed with
   kitchen string

SAUCE:
½ cup chicken broth
¼ cup Madeira wine
1 cup fresh or frozen
   cranberries
⅓ cup sugar
1 teaspoon fresh thyme
Thyme sprigs for garnish

Adjacent woodland area near the bogs of the Federal Furnace Cranberry Company.

John K. Robson photograph

Pan-Seared Ostrich Steaks with Cranberry Orange Rosemary Sauce

MAKES 4 SERVINGS

4 ostrich steaks
2 tablespoons olive or
    vegetable oil
½ cup chicken broth
¼ cup Port wine
2 tablespoons orange juice
½ teaspoon orange zest
¾ cup homemade or canned
    whole berry cranberry
    sauce
1 teaspoon fresh rosemary
Rosemary sprigs for garnish

Ostrich is gaining popularity as a low-fat, high protein red meat alternative. It is delicious in its own right and easily adapts to many flavorings. Because ostrich contains so little fat, it is best served medium to medium rare and cooked quickly at a high temperature.

Heat the oil in a sauté pan large enough to hold the four ostrich steaks. When the oil is hot, sear the ostrich steaks on both sides for 6-10 minutes. When the steaks are done, transfer them to a plate to keep warm. Keep the pan on medium heat and deglaze the pan with ½ cup chicken broth, scraping well to get all the bits off the bottom of the pan. Add the Port, orange juice and the cranberry sauce. Whisk to combine the sauce into the liquid. Bring the sauce to a boil. Add the orange zest and the rosemary. Simmer for 5 minutes or until the sauce has thickened. Pour any juices that may have accumulated under the steaks into the sauce. To serve, place one steak on each plate. Put a sprig of fresh rosemary on the steak, and serve some sauce to the side of the steak. Fresh vegetables and roasted or mashed potatoes would go nicely with this.

Sautéed Chicken in Cranberry Balsamic Vinegar Sauce

SERVES 6 • RECIPE CAN EASILY BE HALVED

3 tablespoons butter
2 cups chopped onions
½ cup chicken broth
1 pound white or brown
    mushrooms, sliced
3 tablespoons balsamic
    vinegar
1 cup whole cranberry sauce
    (8-ounce can)
2 tablespoons olive oil
4 pounds chicken breasts and
    thighs

Melt the butter in a large skillet or Dutch oven. Add the onions and cook on medium heat until they begin to soften, about 5 minutes. Add the mushrooms. Continue to cook until they soften, about five minutes. Remove the mushrooms and onions from the pan and place on a plate. In a mixing bowl, whisk together the chicken broth, the cranberry sauce and the vinegar. Heat the olive oil in the skillet. Add the chicken and cook on medium heat. Brown the chicken on all sides, turning each piece to cook evenly, about 15 minutes. Pour in the cranberry mixture. Bring to a boil. Reduce the heat to a simmer. Cover and simmer the chicken for 10 minutes, turning the pieces over every few minutes. Add the mushrooms and onions. Cover and simmer for another 10 minutes. Continue to turn the pieces of chicken over to cook evenly. Uncover and continue to simmer for 5-10 minutes, stirring frequently until the chicken is done. Serve with rice, pasta or polenta.

Roast Saddle of Venison with Cranberry Essence and Celery Root Puree

SERVES 6-8

Preheat oven to 450°.

Wipe the venison with a damp cloth. Bring a large sauté pan to medium heat and add the oil. When the oil is heated, add the meat and sear on both sides. Roast the meat in a 450° oven 5 minutes for rare, or 8 minutes for medium. Remove the roast from the oven and let rest on a rack. Season with salt and pepper. Deglaze the roasting pan with the stock, scraping well to get all the bits off the bottom of the pan. Place the juices from the roasting pan in a small pot. Add the veal, chicken or *Venison Demi-Glace*, cranberries and the butter. Bring to a boil so the berries pop and give their flavor to the *Demi-Glace* sauce.

FOR THE VENISON DEMI-GLACE:

Heat the oil in a heavy pot and brown meat evenly on all sides. Remove the browned meat, and pour out the remaining fat. Add the stock and tarragon to the pan and deglaze the pan well. Reduce the liquid by half and strain.

FOR CELERY ROOT PUREE:

In a heavy pot, combine the chicken stock, water, nutmeg, celery root, potato and garlic. Bring to a boil. Lower the heat and let the vegetables simmer until they are tender, about 15 minutes. Strain the cooked vegetables, reserving the cooking liquid. Puree them through a food mill or in a food processor. Add the cream and some of the cooking liquid to adjust the consistency. Reheat gently to serve.

TO SERVE:

Spoon some of the *Celery Root Puree* in the center of each warmed plate. Place 2-3 slices of venison on top of the puree. Finish with the *Demi-Glace* and garnish with a tarragon sprig.

— *Rebecca Ets-Hokin, Tiburon, CA*

Mahlon Stacey, an early American settler, wrote to his brother in England in 1689 that "an excellent sauce is made of them for venison, turkeys and other great fowl."

1 three-pound boned saddle of venison
1 tablespoon grapeseed oil (or corn or vegetable oil)
Coarse sea salt
Freshly ground pepper
¼ cup veal or chicken stock
2 cups veal, chicken or venison demi-glace *
½ cup chopped fresh or frozen cranberries
1 tablespoon unsalted butter
Tarragon sprigs for garnish

TO MAKE VENISON DEMI-GLACE:

1 pound venison, fat removed and cut into ½-inch cubes
1 tablespoon grapeseed oil
4 cups veal or chicken stock
1 sprig tarragon

TO MAKE CELERY ROOT PUREE:

3 cups chicken stock
4 cups cold water
¼ teaspoon freshly ground nutmeg
1 pound celery root, peeled and cut into large cubes
1 large baking potato, peeled and cut into large cubes
1 garlic bulb, skins removed
⅛ cup cream
Sea salt to taste

* *The* Venison Demi-Glace *can be substituted with commercially prepared veal or chicken demi-glace, sold in gourmet cooking stores or fine markets.*

Chapter Five

....

Desserts

Baked Apples with Spiced Cranberries

4 large baking apples
1 cup chopped fresh or frozen
 cranberries
¼ cup brown sugar
¼ cup white sugar
2 teaspoons ground cinnamon
½ teaspoon ground clove
½ teaspoon ground nutmeg
½ cup orange juice

Baked apples are a common American favorite. The cranberries bring a unique flavor and color to this recipe. Cooking them in the microwave oven makes this recipe even easier, and the apples stay plump and moist.

Core each apple, leaving a good-sized opening. Peel a 1" strip all around the top of each apple. Place the apples in a microwave safe baking dish. In a small bowl combine the cranberries, brown sugar, white sugar, cinnamon, clove and nutmeg. Fill each apple with an equal amount of the cranberry mixture. Pour any extra into the bottom of the baking dish. Pour the juice into the bottom of the dish. Cover tightly with plastic wrap. Cook on HIGH for 6 minutes. Uncover the wrap and rotate the apples a half turn. Cook on HIGH for another 5 minutes. Let stand, covered for 10 minutes. Serve warm with cooking juices.

This recipe can also be prepared in a conventional oven. Prepare apples following the directions. Cover with aluminum foil. Bake in a preheated 350° oven for 50-60 minutes or until apples feel soft.

Serve as a side dish with pork, lamb or poultry, or as a dessert alone or served with a dollop of *crème fraiche,* whipped cream, fresh or frozen yogurt or ice cream.

You can use dried cranberries instead of fresh or frozen. Just reduce the sugar by half the amount. Follow the same directions.

As wild cranberries became more commonly collected and used, the desire for a more abundant cranberry harvest became linked to an interest in commercial cultivation. In 1829, soon after cranberries began being commercially cultivated, a later American cookbook was published, The American Frugal Housewife. *It was aimed at "...those who are not ashamed of economy."*

Boiling cranberries into sauce at Ocean Spray Cranberries, 1948.

Ocean Spray Cranberries photograph

Cranberry Applesauce

MAKES 4 CUPS

This side dish is lovely with pork, poultry or game. It adds color and texture.

Place all the ingredients in a 3-4 quart saucepan. Bring to a boil and cook over a low heat, covered, until the cranberries have popped and the apples are soft, approximately 15-20 minutes. Place the applesauce in a food processor and blend until smooth. Serve warm or chilled.

4 large cooking apples, peeled, cored, and cut into chunks
1 cup fresh or frozen cranberries
¾ cup sugar
1 cup water
¼ teaspoon ground clove
½ teaspoon ground cinnamon

Some historians suggest that the slender stem and the downward hanging blossom, resembling the head and neck of an English crane, gave rise to the name "crane-berry," later shortened to "cranberry."

Cranberry Raspberry Slump

SERVES 6-8

Cranberry Raspberry Slump (photo page 74)

Slumps, grunts, buckles, bettys and pandowdies date back to the very beginnings of colonial New England cooking. All are simple, yet elegant fruit desserts, made with ingredients available seasonally. They are all variations on a theme: sweetened fresh fruits topped with a crust or dough, cooked and served with sweet cream. Culinary historians generally agree that slumps are baked desserts. But do "slumps" slump? This one does.

Preheat oven to 400°.

Butter a 2 quart baking dish. In a large bowl combine the cranberries, raspberries, sugar and water. Place in the baking dish. Place the dish in the oven to heat the fruit for 20 minutes if fresh or 25 minutes if frozen. Take the dish out of the oven. The fruit will be liquidy. In a mixing bowl combine the flour, baking powder, salt and sugar. Slowly add the butter and milk to the flour mixture, stirring as you do. The batter will be a bit lumpy. Do not over mix, as over mixing will toughen the batter.

Spoon the batter over the hot berries. Bake 20-25 minutes until the top has lightly browned. Serve with cream or ice cream.

Adapted from a recipe by Drew Spangler, Mill Valley, CA

FOR THE FRUIT:
2 cups whole fresh or frozen cranberries
2 cups fresh or frozen raspberries
1 cup sugar
½ cup water

FOR THE BATTER:
1½ cups all-purpose flour
2 teaspoons baking powder
⅛ teaspoon salt
¼ cup sugar
¼ cup (½ stick) butter, melted
¾ cup milk

Pear and Cranberry Bread Pudding

SERVES 12

FOR THE CUSTARD:
1 cup milk
⅔ cup butter, room
    temperature
½ cup sugar
6 eggs
1 teaspoon ground cinnamon
3 tablespoons brandy or vanilla

FOR THE FRUIT:
4 ripe pears
⅛ cup cinnamon–sugar
2 tablespoons butter

FOR THE STREUSEL TOPPING:
½ cup granulated sugar
½ cup brown sugar
1 cup (2 sticks) butter cut into
    chunks
2 cups all-purpose flour
2 teaspoon ground cinnamon
1 teaspoon vanilla

FOR THE BREAD PUDDING:
1½ pounds bread (challah,
    brioche or other egg bread
    works well), cut into 1-inch
    cubes
1½ cups whole fresh or frozen
    cranberries
2 cups heavy cream

TO MAKE THE CUSTARD:

Scald the milk. Set it aside. In an electric mixer cream the butter and the sugar together. Add the eggs, one at a time until they are fully incorporated. Add the milk. Once the mixture is well combined, add the cinnamon and the brandy. Set this mixture aside.

TO PREPARE THE PEARS:

Peel, core and slice the pears into thin slices. Toss the pears in the cinnamon-sugar. In a small skillet, heat the butter on medium high heat. Add the pears and cook until they are caramelized and tender, about 5-10 minutes. Set the pears aside.

FOR THE STREUSEL TOPPING:

In a mixing bowl combine the sugars and butter until the butter pieces are coated with sugar and the mixture is crumbly. Add the flour, cinnamon and vanilla. Continue to combine the ingredients until the mixture resembles pea-sized pieces of butter. Do not over mix. You want this to be crumbly, not creamed. Set aside.

TO ASSEMBLE THE BREAD PUDDING:

Preheat oven to 350°.

Butter generously a 6 quart souffle dish with high sides or a deep lasagne pan. Spread half of the cubed bread evenly along the bottom of the dish. Distribute all the caramelized pears over the bread layer. Sprinkle the cranberries evenly over the pears. Pour half of the custard mixture over the fruit. Spread the rest of the bread over the custard. Pour the rest of the custard mixture over the bread. Finally, pour the cream over the top. Sprinkle the streusel topping evenly over the bread pudding. Cover with foil and bake for 25 minutes. Uncover and continue to bake for another 25 minutes or until golden brown and the pudding is set in the middle.

— *Jamie Currier, Pastry Chef, Left Bank Restaurant, Larkspur, CA*

By the mid-1800s American cranberries were being shipped overseas

to England. Cranberries had become a distinctively American fruit

and new hallmark of American cuisine. "Cranberry Fever", as it

came to be known, was here to stay.

Cranberry Apple Grunt

SERVES 6-8

How did a "grunt" get its name? One story is that "grunt" refers to the sound of satisfaction heard after eating one. Regardless of the origin of the name, culinary historians generally agree that grunts are always steamed. They are an old fashioned New England dessert of fruit, usually some form of berries, topped with a biscuit dough. Unlike a cobbler, which is a deep dish fruit topped with a biscuit and baked, grunts are stewed or steamed. A grunt is also recognized as a dumpling, and many recipes for grunts and dumplings are quite similar.

Sift the flour, baking powder, salt and sugar together into a mixing bowl. Add the egg and cream alternately, stirring gently to form a smooth dough. Do not over mix, as over mixing will toughen the dough. Set aside.

Put the apples, cranberries, sugars, water and cinnamon in a large sauté pan or Dutch oven. Bring to a boil. Reduce to a simmer. Simmer for 5 minutes, stirring as it cooks. Drop the dough by the tablespoonful onto the fruit mixture, spacing the dumplings about 1" apart. You should have enough dough to make 6-8 dumplings. Cover and continue to simmer undisturbed for 15 minutes. The dumplings will puff up when done, and a toothpick inserted into one will come out clean.

To serve, place the dumplings in individual bowls and spoon the fruit mixture around them. Serve with cream or ice cream.

— Adapted from a recipe by Drew Spangler, Mill Valley, CA

FOR THE TOPPING:
1 cup all-purpose flour
2 teaspoons baking powder
¼ teaspoon salt
2 tablespoons sugar
1 egg, beaten
½ cup light cream

FOR THE FRUIT:
4 cups apples, peeled, cored
    and sliced ¼ inch thick
    (about 3 large)
2 cups whole cranberries, fresh
    or frozen
⅔ cup brown sugar
⅔ cup granulated sugar
½ cup water
1 teaspoon ground cinnamon

The first known cranberry bog was planted in 1846 by Captain Alvin Cahoon in the Pleasant Lake area of Harwich. His cousin and neighbor, Captain Cyrus Cahoon, also began developing bogs and together the two men experimented and developed methods of cultivation that gave a foundation to the young industry. Within ten years, the total cranberry land on Cape Cod was 1,074 acres, with Harwich the leader.

Water-reel harvesting near Pleasant Lake in Harwich, Cape Cod, MA.

Joseph D. Thomas photograph

Tarte Tartin with Caramelized Cranberries

SERVES 8-10

BASIC SHORT PASTRY:

1½ cups all-purpose flour

½ teaspoon salt

4 ounces unsalted butter, cut into 1" pieces and chilled

½ teaspoon fresh lemon juice

4-6 tablespoons ice water

TARTE TARTIN:

1¼ cups sugar

4-5 cups tart apples (about 4 apples) peeled, cored and sliced

½ cup chopped fresh or frozen cranberries

4 tablespoons butter

Preheat oven to 375°.

In a food processor or by hand combine the flour and salt. Work the butter into the flour until the mixture is crumbly.

Add the lemon juice and then the water gradually, mixing lightly until the dough gathers together. Flatten the dough, sprinkle with a little flour, wrap in plastic, and allow to rest in the refrigerator for 1 hour before rolling out. Put 1 cup of the sugar in a small, heavy saucepan and cook over medium-high heat. Swirl the pan slowly by its handle. Do not stir. The sugar will melt into a liquid. The liquid will come to a boil. Continue to swirl the pan as the liquid boils and turns clear. Boil for several minutes, continuing to swirl the pan until the sugar turns a nice caramel brown color. Take the pan off the heat immediately. Pour the caramel into the bottom of an 8"-9" cake pan, tilting the pan so the caramelized sugar coats the bottom and sides. Sprinkle the cranberries over the caramel. Lay the apple slices over the cranberries. Sprinkle with the remaining ¼ cup sugar and dot with the butter. Roll out the pastry about ¼" thick and about 2" larger than the cake pan. Lay the pastry on top of the apples, tucking it in around the edges. Bake the tart for 50-55 minutes until the crust is golden brown. Allow the tart to cool for one hour. Then turn it out onto a serving platter, so that the crust forms the base, with the cranberries on top. Serve warm or at room temperature.

— *Adapted from a recipe by Rebecca Ets-Hokin, Tiburon, CA*

The six-quart measure, used by handpickers circa 1880–1940.
—Illustration by Robert A. Henry

Screening method used at Ocean Spray, 1989.

At the screening area at Ocean Spray's receiving station in South Carver, berries are run through a barrel-washer and a stick-remover and then pass along a conveyor that grades them by allowing the smaller ones to fall through the grate. At the end of the conveyor, two brushes turning in opposite directions force the soft berries through and into a bin.

Joseph D. Thomas photograph

Blueberry Cranberry Cobbler

SERVES 8

This traditional American dish can be made with any number of fruit combinations. The blueberries, another native American fruit, pair nicely with the cranberries. Served with vanilla ice cream, this dessert is an all American favorite!

Preheat oven to 425°.

In a medium saucepan combine the cranberries, water and sugar. Bring to a boil and simmer for 5 minutes or until the cranberries just begin to pop. Add the blueberries and lemon juice and bring back to a simmer. Gently stir in the cornstarch and simmer for 5 minutes until the fruit has softened. Set the fruit aside. Prepare the dough by combining the flour, sugar, baking powder and salt in a mixing bowl. Make a well in the center and add about ¾ cup of the half-and-half, a little at a time, until a dough is formed. Knead the dough gently several times on a lightly floured surface and roll it out to 1" thickness. Cut out 8 biscuits in any shape. Pour the fruit into a greased 1½ quart baking dish. Arrange the biscuits on top of the fruit. Brush each biscuit with the remaining half-and-half and sprinkle each with ¼ teaspoon sugar. Bake the cobbler in the middle of the oven for about 15-20 minutes or until the biscuits are golden brown and the fruit is bubbling.

Serve warm with ice cream or fresh whipped cream.

FOR THE COBBLER FILLING:
2 cups whole cranberries, fresh or frozen
¾ cup water
¾ cup sugar
4 cups blueberries
2 teaspoons fresh lemon juice
1 tablespoon cornstarch

FOR THE BISCUIT DOUGH:
2 cups all-purpose flour, sifted
3 tablespoons sugar
2½ teaspoons baking powder
½ teaspoon salt
1 cup half-and-half
2 teaspoons sugar for the biscuit tops

Cranberry Oat Bars

MAKES 18 BARS

Preheat oven to 350°.

In a medium bowl cream the butter, sugar and orange juice. Add the salt and soda, mixing well. Add the oats and flour. Blend the mixture well. Grease a 9" x 12" baking dish. Press half the mixture evenly into the dish. Spread the *Cranberry Raspberry Sauce* evenly over it. Press the remaining flour-oatmeal mixture evenly on top of the sauce. Bake in the oven 45 minutes or until the top layer is golden brown. Cool in the pan on a wire rack. Cut into bars.

¾ cup butter (1½ sticks), softened
¾ cup brown sugar
2 tablespoons orange juice
¼ teaspoon salt
¼ teaspoon baking soda
2 cups rolled oats
1½ cups all-purpose flour
2 cups *Cranberry Raspberry Sauce* (page 43)

Cranberry-Apple Crisp

SERVES 10

6 Granny Smith apples

3 cups (12-ounce bag) fresh
  cranberries

Juice of 1 lemon (about 3
  tablespoons)

1 cup white sugar

1 cup white flour

1 cup rolled oats

1 cup packed dark or light
  brown sugar

1 teaspoon ground cinnamon

½ cup butter

Cranberry-Apple Crisp (photo page 66)

A Thanksgiving favorite! Every year I make this dessert at home for my family and at school with my students. It is so easy and so delicious. Even five-year-olds can help with this one! It's a "No Fail" recipe! Although my husband, Bob, prefers this eaten plain, or with ice cream on a separate dish so it doesn't touch the crisp, I prefer to eat this with a scoop of rich vanilla ice cream on top!

Preheat oven to 350°.

Lightly grease a baking dish or casserole approximately 9" x 13". Core, peel and thinly slice the apples. Rinse the cranberries under cold water, discarding any bad ones. Drain well. In a bowl mix the apples, cranberries, lemon juice, white sugar and ½ cup of the flour. Gently toss until fruit is slightly coated. In a separate bowl combine the oats, brown sugar, remaining ½ cup flour and the cinnamon. Cut in the butter until the mixture is crumbly. Place the fruit into the baking dish. Press the oat mixture topping evenly over the fruit. Cover with foil and bake for 30 minutes. Uncover and continue to bake for another 30 minutes or until the apples are tender, the cranberries are bubbly and the topping has lightly browned. Serve with vanilla ice cream, vanilla frozen yogurt or fresh whipped cream.

Cranberry Nut Tart (photo page 75)

Cranberry Nut Tart

3 large eggs

1 cup brown sugar

½ cup light corn syrup

1 teaspoon vanilla

¼ cup butter, melted

1 tablespoon flour

¼ teaspoon salt

1¼ cups walnuts, hazelnuts or
  pecans, lightly roasted and
  coarsely chopped

3 cups whole fresh or frozen
  cranberries

One 9-10 inch pie crust (see
  Pate Sucree (page 109) **or** *Basic
  Pie Crust* (page 110)

This tart is as beautiful to look at as it is to eat. The cranberries on the top of the tart remain red, whole and shimmer in the glaze. The tart is a bit like a pecan pie filled with mixed nuts and whole cranberries. It makes a stunning holiday dessert.

Preheat oven to 425°.

In a large mixing bowl whisk together the eggs, brown sugar, corn syrup, vanilla and butter. Add the flour and salt and stir until the mixture is smooth. Stir in the nuts, and gently fold in the cranberries. Bake the pie crust in the middle of a 425° oven for 10 minutes. Remove the crust from the oven and let it cool for 10 minutes. Lower oven to 350°. Pour the cranberry-nut mixture into the crust and bake for 45-50 minutes or until the crust is golden and the tart has set. Cool on a rack. Serve warm or at room temperature, either plain or with ice cream or whipped cream. This tart can be made a day in advance and stored covered at room temperature.

Northern Atlantic Coast Cranberry Blackberry Buckle

SERVES 8

This version of a traditional "buckle" has been adapted from recipes from New Brunswick, Canada, along the coast of Maine to southern Massachusetts. Blueberries, boysenberries, nectarines, peaches, or other seasonal fruits can be used. The preparation time is so short that you can have this delicious cake for breakfast, tea time or dessert within one hour.

Preheat oven to 350°.

Cream together the butter and the sugar. Add the egg. Sift together the flour, baking powder and salt. Add the dry ingredients to the wet ingredients. Stir in the milk to make a smooth batter. Pour into a greased 9" x 12" or 9" square pan. Cover the batter with the blackberries and cranberries.

In a small bowl cream together the butter and sugar. Add the flour and cinnamon. Sprinkle the mixture over the berries. Bake in a 350° oven for 50 minutes or until the topping is crisp and golden brown and a toothpick inserted into the cake comes out clean. Serve warm or at room temperature. Serve plain or with whipped cream.

FOR THE CAKE BATTER:
¼ cup (1/2 stick) unsalted butter, softened
½ cup sugar
1 egg, beaten
1 cup all-purpose flour
1½ teaspoons baking powder
⅛ teaspoon salt
⅓ cup milk
1 cup fresh or frozen blackberries
1 cup fresh or frozen chopped cranberries

FOR THE TOPPING:
¼ cup unsalted butter, softened
⅔ cup granulated sugar
⅓ cup all-purpose flour
1 teaspoon cinnamon

Lemon Cranberry Squares

MAKES 18 SQUARES

Preheat oven to 350°.

FOR THE CRUST:

In a food processor or mixer, combine all the ingredients until the dough holds together. If mixing by hand, you may find it necessary to add 1 tablespoon cold water to help the dough hold together. Press evenly over the bottom of a well-greased 9" x 12" or 9½ x 9½" baking dish. Bake 20-25 minutes or until the crust turns a light golden brown. Take pan out of the oven and cool for 10 minutes.

FOR THE TOPPING:

In an electric mixer beat the eggs. Blend in the sugar, lemon peel, lemon juice and baking powder. Stir in the cranberries. Pour the mixture over the warm crust. Return to the oven and bake about 30 minutes or until the topping has set. Remove from the oven and cool. Sprinkle with powdered sugar. Cut into squares and serve at room temperature.

FOR THE CRUST:
1¼ cups all-purpose flour
½ cup butter, chilled
¼ cup granulated sugar

FOR THE TOPPING:
4 eggs
1 cup sugar
Grated peel from 2 lemons
⅓ cup lemon juice
½ teaspoon baking powder
1 cup chopped fresh or frozen cranberries
Powdered sugar for dusting on top

Cranberry Pecan Biscotti

· ·

MAKES ABOUT 40 BISCOTTI

1 cup sugar

½ cup (1 stick) unsalted
    butter, softened

3 eggs

1 teaspoon vanilla extract

1 teaspoon almond extract

1 tablespoon brandy

2½ cups all-purpose flour

1 ½ teaspoons baking powder

¼ teaspoon salt

¾ cup dried cranberries,
    chopped

¾ cup pecans, chopped

Preheat oven to 300° degrees.

Put the pecans on an ungreased cookie sheet and bake in the oven 5-7 minutes to toast. Stir once during toasting. Take out the pecans and raise the oven temperature to 350°. In a mixing bowl cream together the sugar and butter. Add the eggs, beating them in, one at a time. Add the vanilla and almond extracts and brandy. In a separate bowl combine the flour, baking powder, and salt. Stir the dry ingredients into the wet ones. Add the cranberries and pecans. Form the dough into a ball. On a floured work surface, divide the dough in half. Form each half into a long loaf, about 12" long by 3" wide and about 1" high. Bake each loaf on a lightly greased cookie sheet for 25 minutes or until firm. Remove the cookie sheets from the oven and cool slightly. When cool enough to handle (about 10-15 minutes), transfer the loaves to a clean cutting board. With a serrated knife, cut each loaf into diagonal slices about ½"– ¾" thick. Arrange the slices flat on the cookie sheets. Bake for 10 minutes. Turn each biscotti over and bake them on the other side for 10 more minutes, until both sides are lightly browned and toasted. Cool thoroughly and store biscotti in an air tight container.

— Adapted from a recipe by Linda Stoppoloni, San Francisco

Corralling berries at a bog in Wareham, MA. Because of the shrinking demand for fresh cranberries, which are dry harvested, more than 95% of all cranberries harvested world-wide are water harvested.

John K. Robson photograph

Cranberry Apricot Almond Biscotti

MAKES ABOUT 3 DOZEN BISCOTTI

These low-fat biscotti do not contain any butter. They are crunchy, crisp and delicious, especially dipped in coffee.

Preheat oven to 300°.
Put the almonds on an ungreased cookie sheet and bake in the oven 5-7 minutes to toast. Turn once during toasting. Take out the almonds and raise the oven temperature to 350°. In a mixing bowl combine the sugar, eggs and vanilla. In a separate bowl combine the flour, salt, baking powder and cinnamon. Stir the dry ingredients into the wet. Add the almonds, cranberries and apricots. Form the dough into a ball. On a floured work surface, divide the dough in half. Form each half into a long loaf, about 12" long by 3" wide and about 1" high. Bake each loaf on a lightly greased cookie sheet for 25 minutes or until firm. Remove the cookie sheets from the oven and cool slightly. When cool enough to handle (about 10-15 minutes), transfer the loaves to a clean cutting board. With a serrated knife, cut each loaf into diagonal slices about ½"-¾" thick. Arrange the slices flat on the cookie sheets. Bake for 10 minutes. Turn each biscotti over and bake them on the other side for 10 more minutes until both sides are lightly browned and toasted. Cool thoroughly and store biscotti in an air tight container.

1 cup sugar
3 large eggs
1 tablespoon vanilla
2¼ cups all-purpose flour
¼ teaspoon salt
1 teaspoon baking powder
1 teaspoon cinnamon
¾ cup slivered almonds
¼ cup dried cranberries, chopped
½ cup dried apricots, chopped

At David Mann's Garland Bog in Plymouth, MA, water harvesting is done by air boat. Built in Florida and patterned after the Everglades air boats, Mann had his craft built larger to carry more weight while drawing less water than its prototype.

Joseph D. Thomas photograph

Cranberry Tart

SERVES 8-10

6 cups fresh whole cranberries
(two 12- ounce bags)
¾ cup red currant jelly
1½ cups sugar
2 envelopes unflavored gelatin
Freshly grated peel from one
orange
One 9" tart shell *(See recipes for* Pate
Sucree *or* Sweet Nut Crust, *page 109)*

"I said my prayers and ate some

cranberry tart for breakfast." From

the diary of William Byrd, 1/11

A fresh cranberry tart is one of the oldest American cranberry recipes. Quite simply, a true cranberry tart is a tart shell filled with sweetened whole berries. It is beautiful to look at and has a tangy taste, since the berries have been left whole. The sugar and sweet pastry crust offset the tartness of the berries. As with the Shaker Cranberry Pie, *there are many versions of the* Cranberry Tart. *Thickeners include jelly, cornstarch, tapioca, gelatin or flour. The following recipe remains true to the origins of the tart.*

Combine the cranberries, jelly and sugar in a 4 quart saucepan. Cook over medium-low heat for about 5-6 minutes, or until the cranberries become soft but **do not** burst open. Turn off the heat just before they begin to pop open. You will want the majority of the cranberries to remain whole. Add the envelopes of gelatin to the cranberry mixture. Stir well to completely dissolve. Add the orange peel. Let stand about 20 minutes, stirring occasionally. Pour the cranberry filling into a pre-baked tart shell. Chill for at least one hour or up to one day.

Shaker Cranberry Pie

MAKES ONE 9" PIE

¾ cup sugar
1 teaspoon vanilla
1 tablespoon all-purpose flour
1 cup whole cranberries
1 cup raisins
Two 9" pie crusts. *(See recipe for* Basic
Pie Crust, *page 97)*

A perennial plant, cranberries

grow on low-running vines in

sandy bogs and marshes.

Cranberry pie was a popular Shaker dessert during the nineteenth century. What makes this pie unique is that it combines raisins and cranberries. Unlike a tart, it is baked between two crusts, like a traditional fruit pie. There are many versions of cranberry pie. In some recipes the cranberries are left whole. In other recipes the cranberries are coarsely chopped, finely chopped and even ground and cooked before being placed in the bottom crust. A true Shaker pie does not contain nuts and uses white sugar. Here is a recipe for Shaker Cranberry Pie *as it was originally designed.*

Preheat oven to 350°.
In a large bowl mix the sugar with the vanilla. Add the flour. Add the cranberries and raisins. Mix well. Place the ingredients between two uncooked pie crusts. Bake at 350° for 45-50 minutes or until the crust has lightly browned and the cranberries begin to bubble.

Cranberry "Stuff"

SERVES ONE LARGE CROWD

This recipe comes from my friend and photographer, Diane Smith, who grew up in Minnesota.. Diane writes, "This is a recipe from my great, great grandmother, Caroline who was born in Ogdenburg, Canada, in 1823. Her mother was half Indian, and maybe that's where the recipe came from. Caroline's family moved to New York state, and in 1862 she traveled by covered wagon with her husband and twelve children to Minnesota Territory. When my great grandmother, Abby, was about ten years old, Jesse James and another man stopped at their family's farm house and asked for a drink of water. The family later learned that his band of outlaws had just robbed the Northfield, Minnesota bank. She always remembered him as being a nice looking, polite man. "We wouldn't think of having Thanksgiving without Cranberry Stuff. You can never make too much…there's never been anyone who didn't love it, and it's as good cold the next day as it is hot for Thanksgiving dinner."

TO MAKE THE PASTRY :

Mix the flour and butter to make a crumbly consistency. Add a little of the water at a time in order to form the dough into a ball. *Or,* buy ready made pie crusts in the freezer section and thaw. Roll the dough out thin. Cut the dough into 1" strips.

TO ASSEMBLE PIE:

In a large (1½ quart size) casserole dish lay one third of the pastry strips, crisscrossed, along the bottom and up the sides of the dish, letting them hang off the edges temporarily. In a large mixing bowl combine the cranberries, sugar and flour, stirring gently to coat the cranberries. Spoon half the cranberry mixture into the casserole dish. Add several pieces of butter on top. Lay another third of the pastry strips, crisscrossed, over this layer and add the other half of the cranberry mixture on top. Dot with the remaining butter. Lay the last third of the pastry strips, crisscrossed, on top of this layer and crimp and flute the pastry edges. At this point the dish can be refrigerated, frozen or baked.

TO BAKE:

Preheat oven to 350°.
Just before baking, pour 1½ cups boiling water into the casserole dish. Place the casserole dish on a baking pan, and bake for about 1½ hours. Let stand 45 minutes before serving.

— Diane Smith, Tiburon, CA

BASIC PIE PASTRY
FOR THREE CRUSTS:
2 cups all-purpose flour
1 cup butter, softened
¼ cup cold water

FOR THE FILLING:
1 pound cranberries
1 cup sugar
¼ cup all-purpose flour
**½ cup butter, cut into
 thin pieces**

Harvesting at Windswept Bog on Nantucket Island. Water-reel harvesting machines are called "water beaters" by growers because the reel, usually rotating away from the machine, whips through the vines and beats the cranberries loose.

Joseph D. Thomas photograph

Apple Cranberry Currant Pie
with Crumb Topping

SERVES 8-10

FOR THE FILLING:

5 cups peeled and sliced tart
    apples (about 5 Granny
    Smith apples)
1 cup whole fresh or frozen
    cranberries
⅓ cup currants
2 teaspoons fresh lemon juice
¾ cup sugar
¼ cup all-purpose flour
¼ teaspoon salt
1 teaspoon cinnamon
⅛ teaspoon allspice
⅛ teaspoon nutmeg

FOR THE TOPPING:

⅔ cup chopped walnuts and/
    or pecans
½ cup all-purpose flour
⅓ cup quick cooking oats
½ cup brown sugar
1 teaspoon cinnamon
6 tablespoons butter, room
    temperature
One 9-10 inch *pie crust* (see
    Pate Sucree (page 109) or *Basic
    Pie Crust* (page 110)

FOR THE FILLING:

In a large bowl combine the apples, cranberries, currants, lemon juice and sugar. Add the remaining ingredients, tossing to coat all the fruit.

FOR THE TOPPING:

Preheat oven to 375°.

Mix all the ingredients together to form a coarse meal. Pour the filling into the prepared pie crust. Spread the topping evenly on top of the pie. Place the pie on the bottom rack of the oven and cook at 375° for 15 minutes. Reduce the heat to 350° and continue to cook for 45-55 more minutes or until the topping and crust turn a golden brown. Cool the pie on a wire rack for one hour or more. Serve warm or at room temperature.

The high content of Vitamin C in cranberries became recognized,

and by the mid to late 1800s, cranberries were regularly loaded by the barrel

aboard whaling and clipper ships to prevent scurvy.

At White Springs Bog in Wareham, MA, berries are deposited from the elevator into the truck and spread out evenly in the trailer. The man spreading them blows his whistle for the truck driver to move a few feet forward in order for the berries to be evenly scattered.

Joseph D. Thomas photograph

Pate Sucree (Sweet Pastry Shell)

MAKES ONE 9"-10" PASTRY OR TART SHELL

Put the flour, salt, butter, sugar and egg yolk in the bowl of a food processor with the metal blade in place. Process for approximately 10 seconds, turning on and off rapidly. Add 1 tablespoon of cold water at a time, continuing to process until the mixture changes from coarse meal to a ball of dough. Remove from the processor. Chill for one hour or more. Roll out on a lightly floured board for a pie crust or tart shell. To pre-bake, bake the dough in a 9"-10" pie dish or tart pan in a pre-heated 375° oven for 20 minutes or until golden brown.

This can also be made by hand in a bowl using a pastry blender or two knives.

1 cup all-purpose flour
¼ teaspoon salt
6 tablespoons cold unsalted
 butter, cut into pieces
1 tablespoon sugar
1 egg yolk
1-3 tablespoons cold water

Sweet Nut Crust

Preheat oven to 350°.
In a food processor, an electric mixer, or by hand, mix the nuts, sugar, salt, butter and egg yolk. Add the flour, continuing to mix until well blended. Form the dough into a ball. It can be refrigerated for up to two days. Press the dough into the bottom and sides of a 10" tart pan. Bake for about

25 minutes or until the crust has lightly browned.

¾ cup finely chopped nuts
 (walnuts, pecans, almonds
 or hazelnuts)
¼ cup sugar
Pinch of salt
½ cup softened butter
1 egg yolk
1½ cups all-purpose flour

Receiving berries off the elevator, White Springs Bog, Wareham.

Joseph D. Thomas photograph

Popularity of cranberries grew as Pilgrim settlements became thriving towns in the eighteenth century. Each fall, entire families gathered cranberries to preserve for winter use—the first dried cranberries!

Basic Pie Crust

<u>One 8"-10" Pie Crust:</u>
1½ cups all-purpose flour
½ cup (1 stick) unsalted
    butter, chilled and cut into
    small pieces
¼ teaspoon salt
1 tablespoon sugar
3-4 tablespoons ice water

<u>Two 8"-10" Pie Crusts or</u>
<u>One 8"-10" Double Crust Pie:</u>
3 cups all-purpose flour
1 cup (2 sticks) unsalted
    butter, chilled
½ teaspoon salt
2 tablespoons sugar
6 tablespoons ice water

This pie crust is wonderfully easy to make and can be used right away, refrigerated a few days before using, or frozen for use at a later time.

Preheat oven to 350°.

In a large mixing bowl or food processor combine the flour, butter, salt and sugar. Process until the mixture resembles coarse meal. Add the ice water, one tablespoon at a time, until the dough just holds together. Remove the dough from the bowl and form into a flat round. Wrap the dough in plastic wrap and chill for at least an hour before rolling out.

Follow the directions for the single pie crust. Divide the dough in half. Form each section into a flat round. Wrap in plastic wrap and chill for at least an hour before rolling out.

GOOD FOR PICKING
6 QUARTS
OF CRANBERRIES FOR
F. D. Underwood.
CAHOON.

Voucher for picking 6 quarts (one measure).

A tallykeeper records a measure, circa 1900. In the days of handpicking, workers would fill their pails then pour the berries into boxes or crates near the "shore." The tallykeeper recorded each worker's production and issued vouchers or tickets at the end of the day. Often, workers had to wait until the end of the picking season to cash in their vouchers.

Ocean Spray Cranberries photograph

Cranberry Pumpkin Pie

MAKES 2 PIES

FOR PIE CRUSTS:

Preheat oven to 400°.

Mix the dry ingredients together. Cut in the butter until it resembles coarse meal. Sprinkle the water and liqueur over the mixture and form into two balls. Roll out the dough and line two 9" pie pans with the dough; prick all over. Bake at 400° until light brown, about 10 minutes.

FOR FILLING:

Combine all the ingredients in a large mixing bowl. Pour into the prepared crusts. Bake at 400° for 10 minutes. Reduce the heat to 325° and bake for 40 more minutes.

FOR THE TOPPING:

In a small saucepan combine all the ingredients and cook over high heat for 4 minutes. Cool. Spread evenly over both pies.

— By permission of Nantucket Island Chamber of Commerce

Cranberries were hand-picked until around 1900,

when wooden scoops came into use. Mechanical pickers

replaced scoops by the mid 1950s.

CRUST:
2 cups all-purpose flour
1 teaspoon salt
2 tablespoons sugar
8 ounces butter (2 sticks)
2 tablespoons water
2 tablespoons hazelnut liqueur

FILLING:
1½ cups pumpkin
1 cup sugar
1 teaspoon salt
2 teaspoons cinnamon
1 teaspoon nutmeg
½ teaspoon ginger
1 teaspoon vanilla
2 tablespoons hazelnut liqueur
3 eggs, beaten
1 cup whipping cream

TOPPING:
1 cup chopped fresh or frozen cranberries
½ cup sugar
⅓ cup hazelnut liqueur

Ocean Spray Cranberries photograph

A gang of scoopers hard at work on a bog in Rochester, MA, circa 1960.

Cranberry Crème Brulée

SERVES 8-10

FOR THE CRANBERRY MIXTURE:
5 cups fresh or frozen
   cranberries
½ cup granulated sugar
½ cup firmly packed brown
   sugar
½ cup water

FOR THE CUSTARD:
9 egg yolks
5 tablespoons sugar
5 tablespoons maple syrup
3⅓ cups heavy cream, scalded

Preheat oven to 275°.
Combine all of the ingredients into a 3-quart saucepan and simmer approximately 45 minutes or until most of the liquid is gone. While the cranberries are cooking, prepare the custard.

Beat the egg yolks with the sugar and maple syrup in a mixing bowl. Add the scalded cream gradually, so as not to cook the egg yolks. Allow the custard base to cool and skim off any foam. Put 1-2 tablespoons of the cooked cranberries in 8-10 custard ramekins and fill with custard to just below the rim. Place the ramekins in a hot water bath with a cloth on the bottom of the pan. The water should be ½"-¾" high on the sides of the ramekins. Bake at 275° for 50-60 minutes. The custards should just slightly jiggle when gently shaken. Remove from the oven and allow to cool completely. Top each ramekin with a layer of granulated sugar and brown under the broiler.

— By permission of Nantucket Island Chamber of Commerce

Nantucket Cranberry Upside Down Cake

SERVES 8

2 cups chopped fresh or
   frozen cranberries
½ cup chopped pecans
1 cup sugar
2 eggs, well beaten
½ cup butter, melted
¼ cup milk
1 teaspoon vanilla
1 cup all-purpose flour
1 teaspoon baking powder
½ teaspoon baking soda
¼ teaspoon salt

This cake is an adaptation of what is also known as a Bog Pie, a Cape Cod Cranberry Pie and a Cranberry Walnut Pie. In many of these recipes the cranberry nut mixture is poured into a pie crust and then topped and baked with the cake batter on top. It is then served like a pie.

In this recipe there is not a pie crust—only the cake topping which, when cooled, becomes the bottom layer. The beauty is not only in the color and texture, but in the ease of baking.

Preheat oven to 350°.
Butter the bottom of a 9"-10" glass pie plate or 8" square baking dish. Mix the cranberries, pecans and ½ cup sugar in a bowl. Place the mixture on the bottom of the dish. Mix until smooth the eggs, butter, ½ cup sugar, milk and vanilla. In a separate bowl combine the flour, baking powder, baking soda and salt. Add the dry ingredients to the wet, mixing well. Pour the batter over the cranberry mixture. Bake at 350° for 45 minutes or until lightly browned. When the cake has cooled for at least 30 minutes, place a dish on top of the cake, invert it and loosen the cake from the baking dish to release it onto the plate so the cranberries are on top. Serve warm with a dollop of freshly whipped cream.

Cream Cheesecake with Cranberry Glaze

SERVES 12

This is the richest, creamiest cheesecake you will ever experience. The cranberry glaze adds color and drama to this spectacular dessert.

FOR THE CRUST:

Preheat oven to 400°.

Sift the flour and in a bowl, combine it with the sugar and lemon rind. Add the egg yolk and butter. Combine the ingredients with your hands, adding the cold water if needed to make a light dough. Press half of the dough into the bottom of a 9" spring-form pan. Prick the dough lightly with a fork. Bake at 400° 10 minutes or until lightly browned. Butter the sides of the spring form pan. Set it on the base. When the crust has cooled, press the remaining dough along the sides of the pan, touching the bottom crust.

FOR THE FILLING:

In a mixer, blend the cream cheese, sugar, flour, lemon rind, lemon juice and vanilla until smooth. Add the eggs, one at a time, continuing to beat slowly until well combined. Fold in the cream. Pour the mixture into the crust. Bake in a preheated 500° oven for 10 minutes. Reduce the temperature to 250° and continue to bake for 1 hour more. Cool the cheesecake completely.

FOR THE GLAZE:

Combine the water, cranberry juice, cranberries and sugar in a 2-quart saucepan. Boil on moderate heat for 5-10 minutes or until the cranberries just start to pop open. Add the marmalade. Bring to a boil, stirring to mix the marmalade in thoroughly. Cool completely. Gently pour over the cheesecake. Keep refrigerated until ready to serve.

FOR THE CRUST:

1¼ cups all-purpose flour
⅓ cup sugar
1 teaspoon grated lemon rind
1 egg yolk
½ cup butter, softened
1-2 tablespoons cold water

FOR THE FILLING:

2½ pounds cream cheese
1½ cups sugar
3 tablespoons flour
1½ tablespoons grated lemon rind
1 tablespoon fresh lemon juice
1 teaspoon vanilla
6 eggs
½ cup heavy cream

FOR THE GLAZE:

¼ cup water
¼ cup cranberry juice
1 cup fresh or frozen whole cranberries
¼ cup sugar
3 tablespoons orange marmalade

Cranberry juice as we find it today was not bottled until the 1950s though Eatmor Cranberries wrote a recipe for homemade cranberry juice cocktail, years before. The recipe called for fresh cranberries, water and sugar. Directions included boiling the berries and straining the mixture through cheesecloth before bottling.

Label from a 100-pound cranberry barrel.
— Courtesy of John C. Decas

Cranberry Sorbet

MAKES 6 SERVINGS

4 cups fresh or frozen
   cranberries
2 cups water
2 cups sugar
2 tablespoons lemon juice
4 tablespoons orange juice
Fresh mint leaves or twist
   of lemon or orange for
   garnish

This sorbet has an intense cranberry flavor unlike any sorbet you have ever tried! Serve it as a palate cleanser between courses or as a light and elegant dessert.

In a 2-quart saucepan bring the cranberries and water to a boil. Simmer for 20 minutes. Remove from the pan and puree in a blender. Return the cranberries to the pan and add the sugar, lemon juice and orange juice. Bring the mixture to a boil. Remove from the heat and strain. Freeze in an ice cream maker. If you do not have an ice cream maker, pour the mixture into a shallow pan. Place the pan in the freezer. When the sorbet becomes slushy in a couple of hours, stir it. Continue to freeze the sorbet until it has frozen completely. This will take another 4-6 hours.

To serve, use a small ice cream scoop. Place two small scoops in a glass serving dish garnished with a fresh mint leaf or a twist of lemon or orange.

— Adapted from an old family recipe by Peggy Monroe, Longview, WA

Label from a 100-pound cranberry barrel.
— Courtesy of John C. Decas

Cranberry Apple Sunflower Seed Cake

CAKE SERVES 12

1⅓ cups brown sugar or 1 cup
   honey plus 2 tablespoons
   orange juice
½ cup vegetable oil
2 eggs
1 teaspoon vanilla
2 cups all-purpose flour
1 teaspoon baking soda
1 teaspoon ground cinnamon
½ teaspoon nutmeg
1 teaspoon salt
2 cups chopped fresh or
   frozen cranberries
2 cups peeled and sliced apples
½ cup raw sunflower seeds,
   lightly roasted

Preheat oven to 350°.
With an electric mixer or by hand, cream together the sugar (or honey and orange juice), the oil, eggs and vanilla. Combine the dry ingredients and add to the first mixture. Blend well. Stir in the cranberries, apples and sunflower seeds. Pour the batter into a well greased 9" x 12" baking dish. Bake for 45-50 minutes. Cool on a wire rack.

— Iroquois Cranberry Growers, Wahta Mohawks,
from A Cranberry Cookbook, Plus

Note: This is a very dense, moist and delicious cake. The batter is very thick, and the cake may take an additional 10 minutes or so to bake. The servings look pretty dusted with powdered sugar.

Wampanoag Cape Cod Cranberry Pie

MAKES ONE 9-INCH PIE

The maple syrup and cornmeal make this Wampanoag fall harvest favorite unique and delicious. These combined ingredients have been native to the Woodland Region for hundreds of years.

Preheat oven to 425°.

In a medium saucepan combine the cranberries, water, sugar, maple syrup and salt. Bring to a boil. Add the flour or cornmeal, currants or raisins and orange peel, stirring well to combine. Simmer for about 5 minutes until the cranberries begin to pop. Remove from the heat and stir in the butter. Let the mixture cool for 10 minutes. Place the bottom pie crust in a 9" pie plate. Pour the cranberry filling into the pie. Roll out the remaining dough and slice it into long, thin strips. Arrange a latticework of pastry strips on the top of the filling in a basket weave manner. Crimp and flute the pastry edges. Bake the pie for 45-55 minutes until the crust is golden and the juices are bubbling. Cool slightly on a wire rack. Serve warm or at room temperature. Serve plain or with ice cream or whipped cream.

— Enduring Harvests, *by E. Barrie Kavasch*

3 cups whole fresh or frozen
   cranberries
½ cup water
1 cup sugar
1 cup maple syrup*
¼ teaspoon salt
2 tablespoons corn flour, fine
   cornmeal, or enriched flour**
1 cup currants or raisins
3 tablespoons freshly grated
   orange peel
2 tablespoons butter
Basic Pie Crust for a two-crust
   pie *(page 110)*

* I reduced the maple syrup to ½ cup. It was perfect.

** I prefer the taste of the fine cornmeal or corn flour.

Before the hurricanes of 1938 and 1944 wiped out the crop, nearly 40 acres of wild cranberries grew in the dunes in the Lobsterville peninsula on Martha's Vineyard. The Wampanoag re-cultivated the area and the crop is now strong and still wild.

Joseph D. Thomas photograph

Gladys Widdiss, Wampanoag elder, picks cranberries on Martha's Vineyard on Cranberry Day, 1989. Held on the second Tuesday of October, Cranberry Day is when the Aquinnah Wampanoags harvest the wild meadows near the Gay Head cliffs. Gladys, whose Indian name means "wild cranberry," remembers earlier Cranberry Days: "When I was a girl, before automobile time, we got up before sunrise and started cooking for the lunch two to three days before. It was like a great big picnic. We walked and rode in the oxcart my grandfather owned." Historically, cranberries were used in the home for sauces and baking and were bartered for groceries down-Island or for goods like molasses in New Bedford.
(From Elaine Lembo
in Cranberry Harvest.*)*

Sweetened Dried Cranberries

10 ounces fresh cranberries, sliced in half (about 3 cups)
½ cup pure maple syrup

These slightly tart but delicious dried cranberries are so easy to make. My daughter, Lauren, loves snacking on them any time of day!

Wash the berries and slice them in half. Try to get berries that are all the same size. Pour the syrup over the berries and let them soak for a minimum of one hour. They will be sweeter the longer they are soaked. Drain the berries, saving the liquid for later use. Spread the berries out on a large greased cookie sheet and bake at 180° for one hour. Then drizzle the fruit with the left over syrup, and drain off the excess liquid from the cookie sheet. Bake again for about 2 to 2½ hours at 180°. Cool the fruit on a wooden board, and store in the refrigerator. The berries will become more leathery as they dry. These sweetened dried cranberries will not be as sweet as the commercial kind, and therefore will not keep as well. They also will not be as uniform in color. However, they will retain the original cranberry tartness.

— *Iroquois Cranberry Growers Wahta Mohawks,* A Cranberry Cookbook Plus

John Josselyn, who visited New England in 1638 and 1665, wrote, "Cran Berry, or Bear Berry, because Bears use much to feed upon them, is a small, trayling Plant that grows in Salt Marshes…some perfectly round, others Oval, all of them hollow, of a sower astringent taste…."

Marin County Trail Mix

MAKES 5½ CUPS

½ cup dried cranberries
½ cup raisins
½ cup dried apricots, chopped
½ cup dried apples, chopped
½ cup dried coconut
½ cup peanuts (salted or dry roasted)
½ cup almonds (salted or dry roasted)
½ cup cashews, whole or pieces (raw or roasted)
1 cup M&Ms
½ cup shelled sunflower seeds (salted or dry roasted)

Making trail mix from scratch insures that you will always have just the right combination of fruit and nuts for your personal taste, and it will always be fresh. It's so easy to make! Take it on hikes, bike rides, picnics, to work, to school or anywhere!

Mix all the ingredients together. Store in a tightly sealed container in the refrigerator. The mix will keep fresh for two weeks, if it lasts that long! This recipe is just a suggestion. Substitute other nuts and fruits for any of the above to make your own combination.

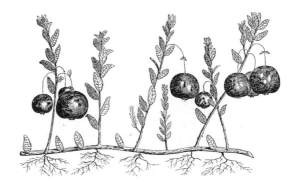

Cherry variety of cranberry.
— *From White:* Cranberry Culture

Cornell Cranberry
Chocolate Chip Cookies

MAKES BETWEEN 3-4 DOZEN, DEPENDING ON SIZE

These tasty treats were created by my daughter Lisa and her friends at Cornell University.

Preheat oven to 375°.
In a large mixing bowl cream together the eggs and the butter. Add the vanilla, brown sugar and white sugar, mixing until smooth. In a separate bowl combine the flour, soda and salt. Gradually stir the flour mixture into the creamed mixture. Stir in the cranberries and chocolate chips. Drop by spoonfuls onto ungreased cookie sheets. Bake for 12-15 minutes or until lightly browned. Remove the cookies from the pans immediately and cool on racks.

Optional: Add ½-¾ cup chopped walnuts to the batter after the chocolate chips. Increase the dried cranberries and chocolate chips to taste.

1 cup (2 sticks) unsalted butter, softened
2 eggs
2 teaspoons vanilla
¾ cup firmly packed brown sugar
½ cup granulated sugar
2¾ cups all-purpose flour
1 teaspoon baking soda
1 teaspoon salt
¾ cup chopped, dried cranberries
One 12-ounce bag semi-sweet chocolate chips

Old-Fashioned Oatmeal Cookies
with Cranberries and Walnuts

MAKES ABOUT 3½ DOZEN

Preheat oven to 375°.
In a large mixing bowl cream the butter with the vanilla and brown sugar. Add the egg, beating until well mixed. Stir in the salt, baking soda and flour. Combine well. Add the oats, then the cranberries and finally the nuts. Drop the batter by tablespoonfuls on lightly greased cookie sheets. Bake for approximately 12 minutes or until golden brown.

¾ cup (1½ sticks) unsalted butter, softened
1 teaspoon vanilla
1 cup brown sugar
1 egg
½ teaspoon salt
½ teaspoon baking soda
1 cup all-purpose flour
2 cups rolled oats
1 cup dried cranberries
¾ cup chopped walnuts

Just picked.

Joseph D. Thomas photograph

Chapter Six

....

Breads, Scones, Coffee Cakes and Muffins

Cranberry Sticky Buns

FOR THE DOUGH:
5 cups all-purpose flour
⅓ cup sugar
1 cup warm milk, 120-130°
½ cup butter, melted
1 tablespoon active dry yeast
2 large eggs
½ teaspoon salt
¾ cup sweetened, dried
   cranberries

FILLING:
1¼ cups packed brown sugar
⅔ cup butter, melted
3 tablespoons light corn syrup
1½ teaspoons cinnamon
½cup chopped pecans,
   optional

This recipe is from the kitchen of Dorothy "Dot" Angley, author of The Full Scoop. *With her husband, she operates Flax Pond Cranberry Farm in Carver, Massachusetts. For years, Dot was in charge of the cranberry recipe contest at the Massachusetts Cranberry Harvest Festival. These sticky buns make a delicious addition to a festive brunch!*

FOR THE DOUGH:

In a large mixer combine 2 cups flour, the sugar, milk, melted butter, yeast, eggs and salt. Beat, scraping the bowl often, until smooth. By hand stir in the cranberries and enough remaining flour to make the dough easy to handle. Turn the dough onto a lightly floured surface. Knead until smooth, about 5 minutes. Place dough in a greased bowl and turn over to grease the other side. Cover the bowl and let the dough rise until doubled in size, about 1 to 1½ hours. Punch the dough down.

FOR THE FILLING:

In a medium bowl stir together all the ingredients. Spread half the filling on the bottom of a greased 9" x 13" baking pan. On a lightly-floured surface, roll the dough into a 9" x 18" rectangle. Spread with the remaining filling. Starting with the long edge, roll it up like a Jelly roll. Pinch the ends into the roll to seal. Cut into 1" slices and place in the pan with filling. Cover and let rise until doubled in size, about 1 hour. Bake in a preheated oven at 375° for 25-30 minutes. Invert the pan on a serving platter and remove pan.

— Dorothy Angley, The Full Scoop

*Cranberry Day, Aquinnah, 1989.
A New England-style clam boil (an Indian creation) is the traditional fare shared by family and friends on Cranberry Day.*

John K. Robson photograph

Note: *This recipe requires around 3 hours for the dough to rise and bake. If you want to make these ahead of time, prepare the buns in the pan. Cover and refrigerate over night. Bring to room temperature for an hour and bake as directed. I used ½ cup butter instead of ⅔ cup in the filling. It was enough. I added ½ cup chopped pecans on top of the filling on the bottom of the pan. If you like nuts, try this crunchy addition.*

The Delaware Indians believed that the cranberry was known

as the symbol of peace. In this function, the great

Delaware Chief Pakimintzen distributed cranberries at tribal peace feasts.

His name came to be associated with the cranberry.

Cranberry Orange Nut Bread

Preheat oven to 350°.

Grease and lightly flour a 9" x 5" loaf pan. In a mixing bowl combine the egg, orange juice and oil. Add the sugar. Combine the flour, baking powder, salt and baking soda. Stir the dry ingredients into the juice mixture. Gently fold in the cranberries, the orange rind and nuts. Pour the batter into prepared pan. Bake 60 minutes or until a toothpick inserted in the middle comes out dry. Cool on a rack for 15 minutes. Remove from pan. Cool completely before cutting.

1 egg
¾ cup orange juice
2 tablespoons vegetable oil
1 cup granulated sugar
2 cups all-purpose flour
1½ teaspoons baking powder
½ teaspoon salt
½ teaspoon baking soda
1 cup chopped cranberries
1 freshly grated orange rind
½ cup chopped walnuts or
    pecans

Zucchini Cranberry Nut Bread

MAKES 2 LARGE LOAVES OR 5 SMALL LOAVES

Preheat oven to 350°.

In a large mixing bowl beat the eggs. Add the oil, orange juice, brown sugar, vanilla and molasses. Beat well. Stir in the zucchini. In a separate bowl combine the flour, salt, baking soda, baking powder, cinnamon, nutmeg and ginger. Add the dry ingredients, a little at a time, to the wet ingredients until well blended. Add the cranberries and nuts. Stir to combine. Grease and flour 2 large (10" x 5") loaf pans or 5 small (3" x 6") loaf pans. Fill the pans ⅔-full with batter. Bake the large loaves for 60 minutes and the small loaves 45 minutes, or until a toothpick inserted in the center of each loaf comes out clean. Cool on a rack for 15 minutes. Remove the bread from the pans and continue to cool on the rack completely before cutting.

During World War II, American troops consumed about

one million pounds of dried cranberries per year.

3 eggs
1 cup vegetable oil
¼ cup orange juice
2 cups brown sugar
2 teaspoons vanilla
2 tablespoons molasses
3 cups grated zucchini
4 cups all-purpose flour
1 teaspoon salt
½ teaspoon baking soda
1 teaspoon baking powder
2 teaspoons cinnamon
½ teaspoon nutmeg
½ teaspoon ginger
1 cup chopped fresh or frozen
    cranberries*
¾ cup chopped walnuts

* If fresh or frozen cranberries are unavailable, substitute with 1 cup chopped dried cranberries and reduce the sugar to 1½ cups.

Zucchini Cranberry Nut Muffins

MAKES 2 DOZEN MUFFINS

Follow the directions for the *Zucchini Cranberry Nut Bread*. Grease two muffin tins. Fill each muffin cup ⅔-full. Bake in a preheated 350° oven 30 minutes or until a toothpick inserted in a muffin comes out clean. Cool in the tin 15 minutes. Remove the muffins and cool on a rack.

Pumpkin Cranberry Bread

MAKES 2 LOAVES

2½ cups sugar

1½ teaspoons salt

3½ cups all-purpose flour

2 teaspoons baking soda

2 teaspoons baking powder

½ teaspoon nutmeg

1 teaspoon cinnamon

¼ teaspoon clove

¼ teaspoon ginger

⅔ cup vegetable oil

1 cup water

4 eggs

2 cups canned pumpkin

2 teaspoons vanilla

1½ cups chopped cranberries
    or 1 cup dried cranberries

¾ cup chopped walnuts

This is another family favorite that seems to disappear as soon as it has cooled! You can double the recipe. It's a lot of batter to work with, but it comes out well. This bread freezes well, so you can eat some now and hide some for later.

Preheat oven to 350°.

Mix together the sugar, salt, flour, baking soda, baking powder and spices. Beat together the oil, water and eggs. Add the pumpkin and vanilla. Mix the wet ingredients into the dry ingredients, stirring until well mixed. Add the cranberries and walnuts. Grease and lightly-flour two bread pans, approximately 10" x 5" x 3". Fill half-full. Bake for 60-65 minutes at 350° or until a toothpick inserted in the middle comes out clean. Cool on a rack for 15 minutes. Take breads out of the pans and cool completely before cutting.

FOR MUFFINS:

Fill two muffin tins and one small loaf pan, half-full. Bake 45 minutes.

— Adapted from a recipe by Gloria Zuflacht, Long Island, NY

Peg-Leg Banana Cranberry Bread

1 large egg

2 ripe bananas, mashed

⅓ cup white sugar

⅓ cup packed brown sugar

1 teaspoon vanilla

½ cup margarine or butter,
    melted

2 cups all-purpose flour

½ teaspoon salt

½ teaspoon baking soda

2 teaspoons baking powder

½ teaspoon cinnamon

1 cup coarsely chopped
    cranberries

Preheat oven to 350°.

In a large mixing bowl beat the egg. Add the bananas, white and brown sugars, the vanilla and the margarine or butter. In another bowl combine the flour, salt, baking soda, baking powder and cinnamon. Add the dry ingredients to the wet, adding a little at a time, blending well. Fold in the cranberries. Bake at 350° for 60 minutes or until a toothpick inserted in the center comes out clean. Cool on a rack for 15 minutes. Remove from the pan. Cool completely before cutting.

Because of his wooden leg, New Jersey cranberry grower John "Peg-Leg" Webb

could not carry his berries down from the loft of his barn where he stored them.

Instead, he would pour them down the steps. He soon noticed that

only the firmest fruit bounced down to the bottom, while the poorest berries

stayed on the steps. His observation led to the discovery of the

cranberry separating machine, which is patented on the "bounce principal."

Good, firm cranberries bounce; damaged, soft berries do not.

Cranberry Corn Muffins

MAKES 1 DOZEN

These muffins are delicious served warm with butter and honey.

Preheat oven to 400°.

In a small bowl combine the butter, egg and milk. In a large bowl combine the sugar, salt, baking powder, flour and cornmeal. Make a well in the center of the flour mixture, and add the egg mixture. Gently stir until the batter is smooth and well combined. Add the cranberries. Pour the batter into a lightly-greased muffin tin, filling each cup ⅔ full. Bake for 25 minutes or until lightly browned and a toothpick inserted in the center of the muffin comes out clean. Cool slightly. Serve warm.

¼ cup melted butter
1 egg, beaten
1 cup milk
½ cup sugar
½ teaspoon salt
1 tablespoon baking powder
1¼ cups all-purpose flour
¾ cup cornmeal
1 cup chopped fresh or frozen cranberries*

* If using dried cranberries, use ¾ cup dried cranberries and ¼ cup sugar.

Easy Cranberry Cornmeal Oat Muffins

These healthy, grainy muffins are great for breakfast and are a favorite of my family. They were inspired by two of my first cookbooks, The New York Times Natural Foods Cookbook *by Jean Hewitt (1971) and* The Tassajara Bread Book *by Edward Espe Brown (1970). These two books introduced many of us to the concept of eating plenty of whole grains and fresh, natural, unrefined, unprocessed foods. Serve these muffins with fresh fruit for a delightful and nutritional start to any day!*

Preheat oven to 350°.

In a large mixing bowl cream the butter or margarine and brown sugar. Add the egg, and mix well to combine. Add the next seven dry ingredients, one at a time, stirring well after each addition. Add the milk and stir well to get a smooth batter. Gently fold in the cranberries. Lightly grease a muffin tin. Pour the batter in each cup, two-thirds full. Bake at 350° for 35-40 minutes. Cool the muffins 10-15 minutes before removing.

Note: The batter can be prepared the night before and kept covered in the refrigerator. Stir in a little bit of milk to thin the batter before filling muffin tin.

½ cup butter or margarine, melted
1 cup brown sugar
1 egg, beaten
¼ teaspoon salt
½ teaspoon baking soda
1 teaspoon baking powder
¾ cup quick-cooking oats
¼ cup wheat germ
¾ cup all-purpose flour
½ cup cornmeal
⅔ cup milk
1 cup fresh or frozen chopped cranberries, *or,* ¾ cup dried cranberries

Corn was the first crop the new settlers learned to cultivate.

The Wampanoags taught them how to plant it on mounds, surrounded by

bean plants and fertilized with whole fish. Corn was a new food for the settlers. It

was not a crop they were familiar with in England. Corn became an

ingredient in many new dishes the new settlers created.

Cranberry Bran Muffins

MAKES 2 DOZEN MUFFINS

3 cups whole natural wheat bran cereal

1 cup boiling water

2 eggs

2 cups buttermilk

½ cup vegetable oil

2½ cups all-purpose flour

1 cup sugar

2 teaspoons baking soda

1 teaspoon baking powder

½ teaspoon salt

1 cup chopped fresh or frozen cranberries*

You may substitute 1 cup dried cranberries for chopped fresh or frozen berries. Reduce the amount of sugar to ⅔ cup. Follow the directions in the same manner.

Preheat oven to 375°.

In a large bowl combine the bran cereal with the boiling water. Mix until the bran has fully absorbed the water. In a small bowl mix together the eggs, buttermilk and oil. Stir into the bran. Add the flour, sugar, soda, baking powder and salt. Combine well. Add the cranberries and gently fold into the muffin mixture. The batter will make 24 muffins. It will keep covered in the refrigerator for up to a week. Before baking, stir the batter and add a little water if it appears to have thickened.

To bake:

Grease a muffin tin and fill the cups ⅔ full with the batter. Bake for 25 minutes or until a toothpick inserted in the center of the muffin comes out clean.

Cranberry box used by New Jersey pickers, 1870. — From White: Cranberry Culture

Cranberry Orange Muffins

MAKES 12 MUFFINS

1 cup chopped cranberries*

¾ cup sugar

1 grated orange peel

2 cups all-purpose flour

2 teaspoons baking powder

½ teaspoon salt

⅓ cup vegetable oil

⅔ cup orange juice

2 eggs

½ cup chopped nuts (optional)

2 tablespoons cinnamon-sugar

If fresh or frozen cranberries are not available, use ½ cup dried cranberries and reduce the sugar to ⅔ cup

Preheat oven to 375°.

Combine the cranberries, sugar and orange peel and set aside. Combine the flour, baking powder and salt in a large bowl. In a small bowl mix together the oil, orange juice and eggs. Mix the wet ingredients into the dry. Stir until just moistened. Add the cranberries and nuts. Spoon batter into lightly greased muffin tins. Sprinkle ½ teaspoon cinnamon sugar on the top of each muffin. Bake about 25 minutes or until golden brown, or until toothpick inserted comes out clean..

— Adapted from a recipe by Joyce Lampert, San Francisco

Cranberry Blueberry Muffins

MAKES 12 MUFFINS

Preheat oven to 375°.
Combine the cranberries, blueberries and sugar and set aside. Combine the flour, baking powder and salt in a large bowl. In a small bowl mix together the oil, orange juice and eggs. Mix the wet ingredients into the dry. Stir until just moistened. Add the berries. Spoon the batter into lightly greased muffin tins, ⅔ full. Sprinkle ½ teaspoon cinnamon-sugar on the top of each muffin. Bake about 25 minutes or until golden brown. Cool on a rack for 5 minutes. Remove from the muffin tins and cool on a wire rack for as long as you can hold out!

¾ cup chopped cranberries
1 cup whole blueberries
¾ cup sugar
2 cups all-purpose flour
2 teaspoons baking powder
½ teaspoon salt
⅓ cup vegetable oil
⅔ cup orange juice
2 eggs
2 tablespoons cinnamon-sugar

Cranberry Applesauce Muffins

MAKES 12 MUFFINS

Preheat oven to 375°.
Combine the cranberries, apples and sugars and set aside. Combine the flour, baking powder, salt and cinnamon in a large bowl. In a small bowl mix together the oil, applesauce, vanilla and eggs. Mix the wet ingredients into the dry. Stir until just moistened. Add the fruit mixture and nuts. Stir until combined. Spoon batter into lightly greased muffin tins. Sprinkle ½ teaspoon cinnamon-sugar on the top of each muffin. Bake about 30 minutes or until golden brown and a toothpick inserted in the center of the muffin comes out dry. If fresh or frozen cranberries are not available, use ½ cup dried cranberries.

¾ cup chopped cranberries
1 cup peeled, cored and diced crisp and tart apples
⅓ cup granulated sugar
⅓ cup packed brown sugar
2 cups all-purpose flour
2 teaspoons baking powder
½ teaspoon salt
1 teaspoon cinnamon
⅓ cup vegetable oil
⅔ cup applesauce
1 teaspoon vanilla
2 eggs
½ cup chopped nuts
2 tablespoons cinnamon-sugar

Cranberry Applesauce Muffins (photo page 67)

Tim Sylvia photograph

It takes about five years from the planting of a bog until the first harvest.

Cranberry Swirl Coffee Cake with Streusel Topping

A form of this popular coffee cake has been a favorite for generations in many families during the holiday season. Friends and family members looked forward to this seasonal treat when cranberry sauce was only available during a few months of the yea.r.

FOR THE COFFEE CAKE:

½ cup (1 stick) butter
¾ cup granulated sugar
2 eggs
1 teaspoon vanilla
1 teaspoon almond extract
2 cups all-purpose flour
1 teaspoon baking powder
½ teaspoon baking soda
½ teaspoon salt
1 cup (one half pint) low-fat
    sour cream
One 8-ounce can whole
    cranberry sauce, mashed

FOR THE STREUSEL TOPPING:

1 tablespoon cinnamon
¾ cup packed brown sugar
¼ cup melted butter
½ cup finely chopped nuts

Preheat oven to 350°.

In a large mixing bowl cream the butter, gradually adding the sugar. Add the eggs, vanilla and almond extract. Blend until smooth. In a separate bowl mix together the dry ingredients. Add the sour cream alternately with the dry ingredients to the creamed mixture. Grease an 8" bundt pan. Combine all the ingredients for the streusel topping and place on the bottom of the bundt pan. Pour half of the coffee cake batter into the bundt pan over the topping. Layer the cranberry sauce evenly over the batter. Swirl the cranberry sauce into the batter with a knife. Pour the remaining half of the batter into the bundt pan. Bake for approximately 55 minutes or until lightly browned. Loosen the edges of the coffee cake with a knife. Turn the pan upside down and cool on a rack fifteen minutes. Loosen the coffee cake from the pan. Serve warm.

Sour Cream Cranberry Coffee Cake

1 cup sugar (instead of ¾ cup)
1 cup fresh or frozen chopped
    cranberries (instead of 8
    ounces of canned sauce)
Add grated zests of one
    orange and one lemon
Powdered sugar for
    dusting on the top

Use the ingredients for the *Cranberry Swirl Coffee Cake* (above) but increase sugar to 1 cup and use fresh or frozen cranberries instead of sauce.

Preheat oven to 350°.

In a large mixing bowl cream the butter, gradually adding the sugar. Add the eggs, vanilla, almond extract and lemon and orange zests. Blend until smooth. In a separate bowl mix together the dry ingredients. Add the sour cream alternately with the dry ingredients to the creamed mixture. Add the cranberries. Grease an 8" bundt pan. Pour the batter into the pan. Bake for approximately 55 minutes or until lightly browned. Loosen the edges of the coffee cake with a knife. Turn the pan upside down and cool on a rack fifteen minutes. Loosen the coffee cake from the pan. Dust with powdered sugar. Serve warm.

Johnnycakes With Chopped Fresh Cranberries

MAKES ABOUT 16 JOHNNYCAKES

Native American tribes of the Woodland Region have enjoyed cornmeal griddle cakes for centuries. Originally made with a flint variety of corn, they were cooked on a hoe or flat board over a fire. Regional and seasonal additions have changed them over time. First known as **ash cakes,** *they were wrapped in cornhusks or grape leaves and baked in ashes at the edges of campfires. They were also known in some areas as* **hoecakes, yokegs,** *or* **nocakes.**

In early colonial times, corn was the principal grain used in cooking, especially in breads. A "johnnycake" was a hard cornmeal pancake, often packed for long journeys or carried out in the field when working for lengthy periods of time. Thus, they were named "Journey Cakes." In New England the word "journey" is pronounced "johnny," perhaps the reason the pancake was re-named **Johnnycake.**

In a mixing bowl combine the cornmeal, flour, salt and sugar. Pour in the water, butter and milk, stirring well after each addition. Stir until the batter is well mixed and smooth. Add the cranberries. Heat butter on a griddle, skillet or frying pan. Drop almost ¼ cup batter onto the cooking surface and cook until small bubbles begin to appear on the surface of the johnnycake, about 3 minutes. Flip cakes over and cook on the other side 2-3 minutes. Serve with butter, maple syrup, *Cranberry-Maple Syrup* (page 48) or jam.

1 cup yellow stone-ground cornmeal
1 cup all-purpose flour
½ teaspoon salt
3 tablespoons sugar
¾ cup boiling water
2 tablespoons melted butter
¾ cup milk
½ cup chopped fresh or frozen cranberries
Butter for frying

The Bell variety cranberry, 1870.
— From White: Cranberry Culture

Cranberry Flapjacks

MAKES ABOUT 20-24 FLAPJACKS

In a large mixing bowl combine all of the dry ingredients. Add the egg and milk. Stir well to mix. Gently fold in the cranberries. Heat a griddle, skillet or frying pan with butter. Pour small circles of the batter onto the hot surface. When the pancakes begin to bubble, flip them over with a spatula and cook on the other side. Butter the pan before cooking each batch. Add a little more milk if the batter thickens while it sits. Serve the flapjacks hot with *Cranberry Maple Syrup* (page 48).

2 cups all-purpose flour
3 tablespoons sugar
½ teaspoon salt
1½ teaspoons baking powder
½ teaspoon baking soda
1 egg, well beaten
1½ cups milk
¾ cup chopped cranberries
Butter for frying

Cranberry Tangerine
Tea Cake with Tangerine Syrup

· ·

MAKES 1 CAKE · 12-14 SERVINGS

TEA CAKE:

2¼ cups all-purpose flour

1 cup sugar

1 teaspoon baking powder

1 teaspoon baking soda

2 cups fresh or frozen
   cranberries

1 cup raisins

2 large eggs

1¼ cups buttermilk

½ cup (¼ pound) butter or
   margarine, melted

TANGERINE SYRUP:

1 teaspoon grated tangerine
   peel

⅔ cup tangerine juice

3 tablespoons lime juice

¾ cup sugar

TO MAKE THE TEA CAKE:

Preheat oven to 325°.

In a large bowl, mix together the flour, sugar, baking powder, soda, cranberries and raisins. In another bowl beat to blend the eggs, buttermilk, and melted butter. Add to flour mixture; stir just until evenly moistened. Pour the batter into a buttered 10 cup plain or fluted tube cake pan. Bake in a 325° oven until the cake is richly browned and begins to pull from pan sides, about 1 hour.

Invert the rack over the pan; holding the rack and pan together, invert the cake onto the rack to release from pan, then tip back into pan. With a slender skewer, poke holes about one inch apart through the cake to the pan. Slowly spoon hot tangerine syrup over the cake, letting the syrup soak in gradually. Let stand at least 6 hours, or cover and chill up to 2 weeks. Invert cake onto a plate and cut into slices.

TANGERINE SYRUP:

In a 1- 1½-quart pan over medium-high heat, combine all the ingredients. Stir often until sugar dissolves and syrup boils rapidly, about 5 minutes. Use hot. If making ahead, let stand up to 6 hours and reheat to boiling.

— *Sunset Magazine, December, 1993*

Note: *The raisins can be deleted. Left-over* Tangerine Syrup *can be mixed with fresh lemon and cranberry juice to make cranberry-tangerine lemonade!*

Upright cutting planting, 1856.
— From Eastman: Cranberry and It's Culture

Cranberry Tangerine Loaf Cakes

· ·

Preheat oven to 325°.

Make *Cranberry Tangerine Tea Cake* batter. Spoon the batter into a large buttered loaf pan (5½" x 9½" / 7-cup) or divide the batter between 2 medium size buttered loaf pans (3½" x 6 " / 2-cup). Bake in a 325° oven until the cakes are browned and begin to pull from the pan sides, about 1 hour for a large loaf and 50-55 minutes for medium size loaves and 45-50 minutes for small loaves. Release and return to pans, poke holes and pour in the *Tangerine Syrup*, or simply cool on a wire rack and slice when loaves have completely cooled.

— *Sunset Magazine, December 1993*

Granola with Dried Cranberries, Cherries and Apricots

MAKES ABOUT 10 CUPS

I have been making granola for thirty years—about as long as the term "granola" was coined. There are endless possibilities for what you choose to make granola with —various grains can be used, and a wide assortment of nuts, seeds and dried fruits can be added. Play with this basic recipe and make it your own—but don't leave out the dried cranberries! They add color, texture, sweetness, nutrition, and, of course, taste!

Preheat oven to 300°.
In a large bowl combine all the grains, seeds, nuts, cinnamon and brown sugar. Stir well to combine. In a small bowl combine the honey, oil and water. Pour the liquid into the oat mixture, tossing the mixture until it is evenly coated. Spread the granola on baking sheets and bake 30 minutes or until golden brown and it sticks together, stirring occasionally to brown evenly. Let the granola cool. Put it in a large bowl and toss in the dried fruit. Store in an airtight container up to one month. Serve with milk and fresh fruit or over yogurt.

5 cups (1 pound) rolled oats
½ cup wheat germ
½ cup oat bran
½ cup raw sunflower seeds
½ cup raw sesame seeds
1½ cups raw cashew or pecan pieces, or sliced almonds
1 teaspoon ground cinnamon
⅓ cup firmly packed brown sugar
½ cup honey
½ cup vegetable oil
½ cup warm water
½ cup dried cranberries
½ cup dried cherries
½ cup chopped dried apricots

Cranberry Orange Scones

MAKES 8-10 SCONES

Preheat oven to 400°.
In a bowl, combine the flour, baking powder, sugar and orange zest. Cut the butter into the dry ingredients until the mixture resembles a fine meal. Add the cranberries. Beat the egg into the milk. Add the liquid to flour mixture, stirring gently. Do not over-mix. Press the dough into a ball and flatten into a round, 1"-thick pie shape. Cut the round into 8-10 pie shaped wedges. Brush lightly with the cream. Sprinkle with the cinnamon sugar. Place the scones on an ungreased cookie sheet spaced 2" apart. Bake at 400° for 20-25 minutes or until lightly browned.

You can freeze the scones after they have been cut into wedge shapes. Brush with the half-and-half, sprinkle with the cinnamon-sugar and freeze.

Cranberry Orange Scones
(photo page 67)

2½ cups flour
1 tablespoon baking powder
3 tablespoons sugar
Grated zest of one orange
½ cup butter
⅔ cup dried cranberries*
1 egg
¾ cup whole milk
3 tablespoons cream (half-and-half)
2 tablespoons cinnamon-sugar

* You may substitute 1 cup whole or ⅔ cup chopped cranberries. Increase the sugar to ½ cup.

Chapter Seven

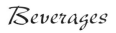

Beverages

California Cranberry Berry Smoothie

MAKES 2 SERVINGS

1 banana
1 cup frozen raspberry low-fat
   yogurt
⅔ cup cranberry juice
½ cup frozen blueberries
½ cup frozen raspberries

*Smoothie
(photo page 79)*

There are many ways to make a smoothie. Experiment with different ingredients until you find the right combination. Try this version for a start:

Combine all ingredients in a blender. Blend. Try using frozen bananas, mango or blackberries and different flavors of frozen yogurt or sherbet.

Cranberry Thai Limeade

SERVES 6-8

8 fresh limes, halved
4 cups water, boiled
¾ cup granulated sugar
pinch of salt
2 tablespoons frozen
   cranberry juice concentrate
6-8 lime slices for garnish
Fresh mint leaves for garnish

Squeeze the juice from the limes. Set the juice and the lime rinds aside. Pour the boiling water into a bowl. Add the sugar and salt. Stir well to dissolve. Add the lime rinds and let the mixture stand for 10 minutes. Squeeze the remaining juice from the rinds into the sugar water and discard the rinds. Pour the water through a sieve into a pitcher. Add the reserved lime juice and the cranberry concentrate. Stir well. To serve, fill a tall glass with ice and limeade. Garnish with lime and a sprig of mint.

Spiced Cranberry Tea

MAKES 4 SERVINGS

2 cups brewed black tea
2 cups cranberry juice
2 teaspoons sugar
4 cinnamon sticks
4 slices orange

This tea is delicious served either steaming hot in a mug or cold over ice as a refreshing iced tea.

In a 2 quart saucepan, combine the tea, cranberry juice, sugar and cinnamon sticks. Simmer for five minutes. Pour the tea into 4 glasses or mugs. Serve with a slice of orange and cinnamon stick floating in the tea. Serve hot or chilled over ice.

MICROWAVE DIRECTIONS:
Combine the tea, juice, sugar and cinnamon in a microwave safe bowl or pitcher. Heat on HIGH for three minutes. Serve as directed.

*Counter-top, display ad for
cranberry juice, circa 1940.
— Ocean Spray Cranberries.*

Spiced Cranberry Cider

MAKES 8-10 SERVINGS

Combine all the ingredients in a 4-quart pot or kettle. Simmer for 5 minutes, stirring continually. Serve hot in mugs garnished with a cinnamon stick.

4 cups apple cider
4 cups cranberry juice
1 teaspoon whole cloves
3 cinnamon sticks
¼ cup packed brown sugar
8-10 cinnamon sticks for serving

Cranberry Spritzer - Non Alcoholic

MAKES A SINGLE SERVING

Add 2 tablespoons frozen concentrate cranberry juice to 6 ounces chilled club soda. *Or,* add ½-cup chilled cranberry juice cocktail to ½ cup chilled club soda. Garnish with a slice of lemon or lime.

— *John Burton, School of Bartending Santa Rosa, CA*

2 tablespoon frozen
    concentrate cranberry
    juice, thawed
6 ounces chilled club soda
Garnish, lemon or lime

There are 44,000 cranberries in one gallon of cranberry juice!

If you strung all the cranberries produced in North America this year, they would

wrap around the earth about forty-five times!

Mango Cranberry Indian Lassi

MAKES THREE 6-OUNCE SERVINGS

Lassi is a simple drink made from yogurt. This nutritious Indian yogurt drink may be the original smoothie. Lassis are enjoyed throughout India. They are especially refreshing on hot summer days. The Lassi in Northern India is flavored with salt and pepper. Try this sweet and tart Lassi on a warm day or as a festive addition to a lunch or Sunday Brunch..

Place yogurt, mango, cranberries, water, honey or sugar and lemon juice in a blender. Blend until the ingredients are fully combined. Add the ice cubes and continue blending until the Lassi is nice and frothy.

— *Drew Spangler, Mill Valley, CA and*
Rekha Dutt, Tiburon, CA and Calcutta, India

1 cup (8 ounces) plain yogurt
½ cup mango pulp (fresh is
    best but canned or frozen
    chunks may be used)
⅓ cup whole cranberries
⅓ cup cold water
5 tablespoons honey or sugar*
1 tablespoon lemon juice
4 ice cubes

You can use both honey and sugar. Honey will give the Lassi a distinct flavor. For tart Lassi lovers, use sugar, and reduce it to 3 tablespoons. For sweet Lassi lovers, increase the sugar or honey to 6 tablespoons.

Poinsettia

2 ounces cranberry juice
6 ounces champagne

In a champagne flute pour in cranberry juice and champagne. *Or*, fill a champagne flute three-quarters full with champagne and the remaining quarter with cranberry juice.

Cranberry Spritzer with White Wine

½ cup chilled white wine
¼ cup chilled club soda
1 tablespoon frozen cranberry
   concentrate, thawed
Garnish, lemon or lime

Stir all ingredients together in a wine glass. Garnish with slice of lemon or lime.

Sex on the Beach

1 ounce vodka
Cranberry juice
Pineapple Juice
Peach schnapps float
Maraschino cherry
Pineapple wedge

In an 11- or 12- ounce Paco Grande (chimney glass) filled with ice, add vodka. Fill with equal parts cranberry juice and pineapple juice. Stir in peach schnapps float. Serve with a Maraschino cherry, pineapple wedge and a long straw.

Cosmopolitan

1 ounce vodka
½ ounce Contreau or
   triple sec
½ ounce Rose's lime juice
2 ounces cranberry juice
Lime wheel for garnish

In an ice-mixing glass or shaker, combine all ingredients except for garnish. Shake or stir. Serve neat. Lime wheel optional.

Water-reel harvester sits idle while workers corral berries at a White Springs Bog in South Carver.

Joseph D. Thomas photograph

Cape Cod

In a 7-ounce highball glass filled with ice, add 1 ounce vodka. Fill with cranberry juice.

Cape Codder

Make a Cape Cod. Serve with a wedge of lime.

Sea Breeze

In a 7-ounce highball glass filled with ice, add 1 ounce vodka. Fill with equal parts cranberry juice and grapefruit juice

Hawaiian Breeze or Bay Breeze

In a 7-ounce highball glass filled with ice, add 1 ounce vodka. Fill with equal parts cranberry juice and pineapple juice.

Advertisement, circa 1940. When the juice cocktail was introduced in the early 1930s, it was touted for its health value. On the verso of this display card we are informed: "Especially for those suffering from indigestion, gastric disorders and for invalids and convalescents whose digestive systems have become sluggish."

Madras

In a 7-ounce highball glass filled with ice, add 1 ounce vodka. Fill with equal parts cranberry juice and orange juice.

— All alcoholic drinks on pages 134-135, courtesy of John Burton, School of Bartending Santa Rosa, CA

In Massachusetts, cranberry bogs such as this one in Rochester, are typically adjacent to thriving wetland areas such as reservoirs, cedar swamps and pine forests.

Cranberries can only grow and survive under a very special combination of factors: they require an acid peat soil, an adequate fresh water supply and a prolonged growing season. Cranberries grow on vines in beds layered with sand, peat, gravel and clay. These beds, commonly known as bogs or marshes, were originally made by glacial deposits. Besides the bog, cranberry growth relies on a surrounding network of support acres—fields, forests, streams and ponds, making up the cranberry wetlands system.

John K. Robson photograph

Appendix

Excerpts from Reports on the Medicinal Value of the Cranberry

UROLOGICAL IMPACT

While trying to account for cranberry juice's unique urinary tract health benefits, Youngstown State University researchers demonstrate that the benefits may be related to the cranberry's ability to inhibit bacteria from adhering to the walls of the urinary tract— thus reducing the risk of infection. The researchers found that 15 ounces of cranberry juice cocktail significantly inhibited the E.coli bacteria, which cause 80 to 90 percent of urinary tract infections from adhering to the urinary tract.

— *Journal of Urology,* May 1984

Tel Aviv University researchers also describe the anti-E. coli adherence property of cranberry juice and attempt to identify the specific components in cranberries that cause this beneficial effect. They conclude that a compound in cranberries of an "unknown nature" prevents certain E. coli from adhering to the bladder's lining.

— *The New England Journal of Medicine,* May 30, 1991

Harvard Medical School researchers conduct the first well-controlled, large-scale clinical trial to demonstrate that drinking cranberry juice cocktail regularly significantly reduced bacteria from growing in the urinary tract. The researchers found that the effect was not due to more acidic urine (the urine of the cranberry juice drinkers was no more acidic than those drinking a non-cranberry placebo drink) and speculated there was something specific in cranberry that prevented bacteria from adhering to the urinary tract. This research was conducted with 153 women (average age 78), using 10 ounces of cranberry juice cocktail, containing 27 percent cranberry juice.

— *Journal of the American Medical Association,* March 9, 1994

In a double-blind clinical trial, researchers from Weber State University find that sexually active women between the ages of 18 and 45 who daily consume a cranberry dietary supplement (from spray-dried cranberry juice) for six months have a significantly lower risk of UTIs than women taking a placebo.

— *Journal of Family Practice,* 1997

Building on the anti-adhesion theory, Tulane University School of Medicine researchers find that cranberry juice actually changes the shape of E. coli. Examining the effects of cranberry juice on the growth and development of E. coli in the lab, researchers found that the hair-like structures that E. coli use to attach to cells in the bladder were inhibited from growing in the presence of cranberry juice. This first visual observation of the change in structure of E. coli vividly showed the power of the cranberry.

— *Journal of Urology,* February 1998

Recurrent urinary tract infections frequently pose a serious problem for hospitalized spinal cord-injured patients. A study conducted with patients compared the effects of drinking plain water or a cranberry juice cocktail. The results indicate that the cranberry juice cocktail significantly reduced bacteria from adhering to bladder cells whereas the water had no effect on bacterial adhesion.

— *Spinal Cord,* January 2001

Rutgers-led scientists identify the active components in cranberries responsible for maintaining urinary tract health as proanthocyanidins or condensed tannins. A daily 10-ounce glass of cranberry juice cocktail will do it.

— "Proanthocyanidins Identified," *The New England Journal of Medicine,* October 8, 1998

DENTAL IMPACT

Research from Tel Aviv University suggests that compounds in cranberries may prevent certain bacteria found in the mouth from adhering to teeth and to other bacteria, apparently through the same type of anti-adhesion mechanism that acts to maintain urinary tract health. These bacteria have been associated with periodontal gum disease. More research is needed to provide an optimal product to deliver this benefit.

— *The Journal of the American Dental Association,* December 1998

IMPACT ON CANCER, THE HEART AND THE STOMACH

Research from the University of Western Ontario studies the effect of daily consumption of cranberry juice and other cranberry products on human breast cancer cell growth in animals. This preliminary research found that cranberry components inhibited the development of tumors in mice injected with human breast cancer cells. More research is needed to understand the benefits to human health.

— The University of Western Ontario, April 2000

Cranberry seeds are found to contain a higher level of tocotrienols, powerful cancer-fighting antioxidants, than in any other plant. Research by Dr. Wasef Nawar of UMass-Amherst reveals that cranberry seed oil contains significant amounts of these potent forms of Vitamin E without the palmitic acid found in other plants containing tocotrienols.

— Internatl. Conference and Exhibit on Nutraceuticals and Functional Foods, September 15, 2000

Early results from an in vitro study suggest cranberry juice might promote cardiovascular health. Cranberry juice proved to be an effective antioxidant, preventing artery-clogging LDL cholesterol from becoming oxidized and thus causing more damage.

— University of Wisconsin LaCrosse, April 2000

Researchers at the University of Wisconsin in Madison test a series of cranberry flavonoid fractions in vitro and find that some of them prevent LDL oxidation. The cranberry proanthocyanidin fraction was highly effective in protecting the LDL from oxidation.

— International Conference on Polyphenols, Freising-Weinhenstephan, Germany, September 10-15, 2000

Researchers at UMass-Amherst discover that cranberry seed oil contains high levels of omega 3 fatty acids and tocotrienols, two compounds rarely found in plants, that are believed to contribute to heart health. Omega 3 fatty acids, usually found in unpleasant tasting fish oil, reduce LDL cholesterol and triglycerides, and tocotrienols are believed to have implications in bloodclotting.

— September 17, 2000 International Conference and Exhibit on Nutraceuticals and Functional Foods

Researchers at the University of Wisconsin-La Crosse discover that compounds found in cranberry extracts dilate blood vessels in rats, thereby reducing their blood pressure. The researchers conclude that the flavonoids and acanthocyanins in cranberry juice may provide the heart benefits of red wine without the alcohol.

— *Journal of Medicinal Foods,* October 2000

Researchers at Tel Aviv University find preliminary evidence that the cranberry may have a similar anti-adhesion effect on H. pylori, the bacteria that are a cause of stomach ulcers. The in vitro study, using human gastric mucus cells and a cranberry fraction, suggests that the cranberry's anti-adhesion effect may prevent the bacteria from attaching to the stomach lining and causing an ulcer. The findings also showed that the cranberry could possibly reverse the adhesion of these bacteria.

— International Conference and Exhibit on Nutraceuticals and Functional Foods, September 15, 2000

Index

Bibliography

Angley, Dorothy. *The Full Scoop*. Carver, Massachusetts: Lady Slipper's Press, 1999.

A Taste of Life: A Fresh Approach to Health, Wellness and Food for Women. Mass.: Ocean Spray Cranberries, 2000.

Bains, Rae. *Indians of the Eastern Woodlands*. Troll Associates, 1985.

Bradford, William. *Of Plymouth Plantation 1620-1647*. Samuel Eliot Morison. New York: Alfred A. Knopf, 1998.

Burns, Diane. *Cranberries, Fruit of the Bogs*. Minneapolis: Carolrhoda Books, Inc., 1994.

Burton, John. *Pour Man's Friend*. California: Apértifs Publishing, 2000.

Cape Cod Cranberry Growers Association. www.cranberries.org

Center for World Indigenous Studies. "The Fourth World Documentation Project." www.night.net/thanksgiving, 1995-98.

Cranberries, The National Cranberry Magazine. December, 1948, Vol. 13, No.8 and January, 1949, Vol. 13, No. 9.

Cranberry Institute. www.cranberryinstitute.org

Eastwood, Benjamin. *The Cranberry and Its Culture*. New York: Orange Judd & Co., 1856.

Erichsen-Brown, Charlotte. *Medicinal and Other Uses of North American Plants*. New York: Dover Publications, Inc., 1979.

George, Jean Craighead. *The First Thanksgiving*. New York: Paperstar, 1996.

Heath, Dwight B. *Mourt's Relation: A Journal of the Pilgrims at Plymouth*. Bedford, Mass.: Applewood Books, 1963.

Hornblower, Malabar. *The Plimoth Plantation New England Cookery Book*. Mass.: The Harvard Common Press, 1990.

Ichord, Loretta Frances. *Hasty Pudding, Johnnycakes, and Other Good Stuff...*. Conn.: The Millbrook Press, 1998.

Iroquois Cranberry Growers. *A Cranberry Cookbook Plus...*Ontario, Canada: Iroquois Cranberry Growers, 1999.

Jaspersohn, William. *Cranberries*. Boston: Houghton Mifflin Co., 1991.

Josselyn, John. *New- England's Rarities Discovered*. Bedford, Massachusetts: Applewood Books, originally published in 1672.

Kavasch, E. Barrie. *Enduring Harvests: Native American Foods and Festivals...*. Guilford, Conn.: Globe Pequot Press, 1995.

Mayflower Web Pages. Caleb Johnson, c 1997. http://members.aol.com/mayflo1620

Nantucket Island Chamber of Commerce. *Nantucket Cranberry Harvest Cookbook*. Massachusetts: Hudson Publishing, 1993.

Nantucket Island of Commerce. *Nantucket Noel Cookbook*. Massachusetts: Hudson Publishing, 1995.

Ocean Spray Cranberries, Inc. Lakeville, Mass.; www.oceanspray.com

Piercy, Caroline B. *The Shaker Cookbook: Not by Food Alone*. New York: Crown Publishers, 1983.

Plimoth Plantation. Plymouth, Massachusetts. www.plimoth.com

Russell, Howard S. *Indian New England Before the Mayflower*. Hanover, NH: University Press of New England, 1980.

Rutgers Blueberry and Cranberry Research and Extension Center, New Jersey.

Simmons, Amelia. *The First American Cookbook: A Facsimile..., 1796*. New York: Dover Publications, Inc., 1958.

Smith, Jeff. *The Frugal Gourmet Cooks American*. New York: William Morrow & Co., Inc., 1987.

Thanksgiving Primer, The. Plymouth, Massachusetts: Plimoth Plantation Inc., 1991.

Thomas, Joseph D. *Cranberry Harvest: A History of Cranberry Growing...*. New Bedford, Mass.: Spinner Pub., 1990.

Wampanoag Cookery. The Children's Museum, Boston: American Science and Engineering, 1974.

Wampanoag Tribe of Gay Head (Aquinnah). Aquinnah, Mass.

Webb, James. *Cape Cod Cranberries*. New York: Orange Judd & Co., 1886.

White, Joseph J. *Cranberry Culture*. New York: Ornage Judd & Co., 1870.

Wisconsin Cranberry Board, Inc. www.wiscran.org

About the Author

Nancy Cappelloni grew up in San Francisco, California. She began cooking as a child and continues her interest in food through teaching children's cooking classes, research, recipe development, and studying enology and food and wine pairing. She is the author of Ethnic Cooking the Microwave Way (Lerner Publications, 1994).

Nancy became interested in the American cranberry and its history following trips to Nantucket, Martha's Vineyard, Cape Cod, Prince Edward Island and Bandon, Oregon. During her research, she took particular interest in Native American cranberry traditions as well as the first accounts of cranberry usage by the early settlers. She has done extensive interviews with many of the people whose lives are impacted by the small red fruit—from Wampanoag elders and Yankee farmers to agricultural scientists and marketing experts.

Nancy and her husband, Robert, and their daughters Lauren, Lisa and Dana, reside in the San Francisco Bay Area. She is an educator in the Marin County School District.

Photograph by Diane Smith